Runes for Writers

Boost Your Creativity and Destroy Writer's Block

Runes for Writers

Boost Your Creativity and Destroy Writer's Block

Marc Graham

Erulian Press | Castle Rock, Colorado
Ancient Tools for Modern Storytellers

Erulian Press
An imprint of Arcadian Dreamscapes LLC
4833 Front Street
Unit B267
Castle Rock CO 80104 USA
www.erulianpress.com

Printed in the United States of America

ISBN: 978-1-7327551-1-6

For my teacher,

Michael William Denney
(Mahadeva)

Also by Marc Graham

Fiction

Of Ashes and Dust
Song of Songs: A Novel of the Queen of Sheba
Son of the Sea, Daughter of the Sun

Non-Fiction

Runes for Writers: An Introduction
Runes for Writers (Cards, Tiles, and Dice)
Thunder Runes (Cards, Tiles, and Dice)

Foreword

STORY IS BIG MEDICINE.
While ancient tribal cultures—and a few today who still maintain their age-old connections—had their shamans, their medicine workers, their magicians and wizards to preserve their myths and legends, the Story of their people, this magic is largely lost to modern society, much to our detriment.

Our myths tell us how the world works, how we—individually and collectively—work within it, and how we can rise toward apotheosis to claim our own positions among the godhead. When we lose those myths, we lose our connection to the natural world, we lose our connection to the worlds beyond the physical, and we lose our connection to one another. Is it any wonder we see such division in our societies?

Today's storytellers are the shamans of modern society. Collectively we have the power, the reach, even the duty to bring to the world transformative stories that transcend the day-to-day, stories that raise human awareness just a little bit higher, and that inspire us to be just a little bit better.

There's no need to be preachy, of course. The most powerful medicine is one the individual doesn't even know he's taking. When we reach into the Realm of Ideas, the Source of Story, and bring back some treasure, some element of primordial magic, then weave a fascinating tale around it, we create the opportunity for upliftment, enlightenment, transformation.

This is the power of Story and of storytellers. I hope this book will be among the tools that empower you in your quest, part of your medicine bag as you bring entertainment and awakening to your readers. May your connection to the Muses, to Inspiration, to that magical realm of Creativity be ever deepened and strengthened. May our stories foster and enable the change we wish—the change we need—to see in the world.

Marc Graham
Ojo Caliente, NM
3 September 2019

Contents

A Quest Begins

Before You Start

T HE NORSE RUNES ARE AMONG the least utilized and most misin-
terpreted of ancient divinatory systems. Their misappropriation
by nationalist and racist groups during the past two centuries has
sullied the Runes' honorable history that spans two millennia or more.
Steeped in the primordial mists of time, the Runes—whose literal
meaning can be interpreted as mystery, secret, or whispering—link
those of Northern European ancestry to our Indo-European kin, and
even further back to our ancient African ancestors. Far from being
symbols of separatist elitism, the Runes stand to remind us of our
shared humanity and origins.

For ease of reading and continuity, I will generally use the descrip-
tor Norse throughout the book when referring to the Runes and
their surrounding culture, history, and myths. Strictly speaking,
the Runes of the Elder Futhark—the subject of this book—derive
from the proto-Germanic period, prior to the division of the tribes
of northwestern Europe into Goths, Danes, Scandinavians, Angles,
Saxons, Franks, or the myriad other groupings. Germanic or Teu-
tonic (literally, of or pertaining to the god Tiw/Tyr) might be better
descriptors of the culture through which the Runes came into being.
However, through the accidents of history and popular culture, most
readers will be more familiar and comfortable with the Norse variety

of myths and language, and I will generally make use of those. The purist may rightly criticize this inaccuracy, and I beg forgiveness for the sake of expediency and a broader reach of the work.

Next, a brief note on style. I tend toward the British in my flair for Capitalization, much to the chagrin of my editors. I'll try to rein it in here, but will tend to capitalize Runes when referring to the shamanic system and the natural energies that underlie it. When referring to individual characters (runestaves), layouts (runecastings), and so on, these will be in the lower case.

As the title suggests, the focus of this book and associated materials is the application of the Runes to storytelling. Since my particular medium is long-form fiction, I will tend to refer to aspects of novel-writing over and above other outlets. However, the uses of the Runes presented in this book are applicable to all forms of storytelling in whatever medium. Moreover, the Runes have a far broader, deeper application to the general navigation of daily life. While this further investigation may be the subject of a future book, the astute reader will glean those elements that have universal import and work them into all aspects of being.

I encourage you to keep a notebook to record not only your rune-castings and interpretations, but to keep track of your insights and inspirations. While I provide a foundation to understanding each of the runes, your experience and intuition will surely build upon that. Rune reading is very much an intuitive endeavor that goes far beyond memorization of flashcards, symbols, and generic meanings. The Runes are shamanic tools, and the more you use them, the more you will strengthen your own shamanic abilities—inherent in all storytellers—which will enable you to better navigate the Realm of Story and life in general.

Join the conversation and share your insights on the Runes for Writers Facebook page (https://www.facebook.com/RunesForWriters).

Who Is This Book For?

T HIS BOOK IS INTENDED TO BE used by experienced storytellers who are ready to boost their creativity, efficiency, and output to the next level.

This book is not about craft. It is not about marketing or building a tribe or how to navigate the publishing world, traditional or indie. There are plenty of excellent books and courses available to provide these fundamentals of the storyteller's journey.

Ideally, the reader will have completed one or more manuscripts, perhaps even have some publishing credits and commercial success. The tools presented here require a strong foundation to build a monument to storytelling higher and grander even than what you've achieved so far.

Beyond considerations of your writing career, getting the most out of the Runes requires a certain open-mindedness, a willingness to embrace (or at least accept) the existence of things beyond what the intellect and senses can reveal. This shouldn't be a great stretch. After all, as a writer you're already a shaman, a wizard, a mage. You reach into the invisible Realm of Story to bring into physical manifestation (and into the minds of complete strangers) something that never existed before.

So, if you have a solid grasp of your craft...

...if you're ready to master a system that brings the joy and fun back to storytelling...

...if you're ready to unleash your full creative potential, then read on, dear friend. This book is for you.

How To Use This Book

THIS BOOK PROVIDES AN introduction to the Norse Runes within the context of the ancient culture of Northern Europe, along with their application to the storytelling process.

These four parts of Runes for Writers will guide the storyteller on a journey of discovery. Part One lays out the premise and function of the book.

Part Two begins the quest with an exploration of the Runes, their history, meanings, sound forms, and interpretations. Even if you're familiar with the Runes, I encourage you to at least peruse this section, as my interpretation of the Rune meanings may vary from what you've encountered before. That said, if you are an experienced rune practitioner, you should rely upon your own revelations as you apply the Runes to your stories.

Part Three presents the practical application of the Runes to storytelling, presenting sample runecastings, interpretations, and story development. This is the heart of the book, where we'll begin to develop the set of shamanic tools to deepen your connection to Story.

Finally, Part Four offers some suggestions for storytellers to take their craft and creativity to deeper levels.

While a proper understanding of and facility with the Runes will come from a cover-to-cover reading, I fully understand the desire to jump right in and start using them. That said, everything the eager, would-be runecaster needs to get started can be found in Part Three, The Journey Back. As the name implies, runecasting itself forms only a small part of this journey into the ancient mystery. Feel free to dive right in. Should you become stuck or confused, or if your curiosity or desire for a deeper understanding grabs hold of you, the remainder of the book will be here to aid your explorations.

As noted earlier, I invite you to share your experiences, interpretations, and specific runecastings—and learn about what others are doing—on the Runes for Writers Facebook page (https://www.facebook.com/RunesForWriters). I hope to see you there!

Seizing the Runes

A (Very) Brief History of the Runes

THE NORSE RUNES SERVED AS the writing system for early Germanic societies for nearly a millennium, from at least 200 CE to 1000 CE. This Futhark—named for the initial characters of the writing system (F-U-TH-A-R-K), similarly to the Latin alphabet (A-B)—was used in documents and inscriptions from the Black Sea to the western coast of Norway.

Prior to this time period, the Roman historian Tacitus (writing about 80 CE) refers to the use of engraved slips of wood in divinatory practices—a likely reference to runestaves. Given the widespread and uniform appearance of the runes, it can be safely assumed that their development, adoption, and standardization extend back into the centuries before the Common Era.

As the proto-Germanic tribes separated and came into contact with different cultures, their languages evolved into German, Norse, Frankish, Anglic, and a half-dozen more. In parallel, the original writing system of the Elder Futhark also evolved to meet the linguistic needs of the developing nations, giving rise to the Younger Futhark, the Anglo-Frisian Futhork, and others.

Over time, the Roman religion supplanted the worship of the old gods, while the Latin alphabet replaced the various Futharks in use across northern Europe. Following the christianization of Iceland, the last bastion of Thor, Odin & company, the Runes were relegated to the status of antiquarian curiosity.

The evolution of the Futhark is still a matter of scholarly debate. The most accepted theory is a derivation from the Phoenician alphabet, via the Greeks or Etruscans. While this theory accounts for some of the similarities in shape of certain characters, it does not explain the order of the characters.

The alphabets developed around the Mediterranean basin and the Near East are all just that—writing systems that begin with A & B (Aleph-Beit, Alpha-Beta, and so on). The Germanic people were nothing if not pragmatic. It makes little sense that they would adopt the writing system of their southern neighbors, only to shuffle up the order into a pattern unique among the world's writing systems. It seems more likely that the order of the sound values (prior to their use in a writing system) was established well in antiquity, and that certain characters may (or may not) have been influenced through contact with neighboring cultures.

It is my assertion that the origins of the Futhark date into prehistory. It is my further assertion (far more speculative) that the Runes themselves are timeless. According to Norse myth, the Runes predate their discoverer, Odin, who himself was responsible for the creation of Midgard, the physical world we inhabit.

Regardless of their true nature and origins, we will see that the Runes of the Elder Futhark—the subject of this book—provide a powerful and highly effective tool for modern storytellers.

The Elder Futhark

THE ELDER FUTHARK CONSISTS of twenty-four characters, which we divide into three rows or aetts (literally, clans) of eight runes each. The numbers 3 and 8 both held (and continue to hold) special significance in Norse cosmology, indeed in the mythic structures of many peoples.

This association makes the Elder Futhark particularly powerful compared to its descendant systems, which ranged from sixteen to thirty-three characters. The symmetry and symbolism of the 8x3 grid hints at the powerful nature of the Elder Futhark far beyond a simple writing system.

The very shape of the numeral 8 hints at its connection to the Infinite. We can relate it to the eight directions of the compass rose. These, when combined with the center point, further correspond to the Nine Worlds of Norse cosmology, the realms of Yggdrasil, the World Tree.

Three is also a highly symbolic number. We divide time into Past, Present, and Future. An individual's life is segmented into youth, adulthood, and old age. Freud theorized the threefold human nature of Ego, Id, and Superego. Many of the world's religions embody the sublime mystery of this number in one holy trinity or another. In the case of the Norse, this triune nature is reflected in the brothers Odin, Ve, and Vili.

Early in the evolution of the cosmos, following the chaotic expansion of the giants—Jotnar, the titanic forces of nature—these three sons of Borr, one of the giants, slew their great-grandfather Ymir, the first individual to emerge from the void of Ginungagap. From his body they created Midgard, what would become our world of physical experience. They made the earth of his flesh, the trees of his hair, the mountains of his bones, and the sky of his skull.

Sometime after the establishment of Midgard, the brothers came upon a pair of primitive lifeforms. Sensing their potential, Vili gave them flesh and bone, Ve senses and emotion, and Odin the breath of life and awareness. Thus, this Norse trinity is associated with the three basic aspects of humanity: Body (Vili), Heart (Ve), and Spirit (Odin).

As we'll see, the 8x3 arrangement of the Runes facilitates access to the source of creativity and has a profound connection to the very nature of Story.

So, let's dive in.

The First Aett

THE FIRST AETT IS ASSOCIATED with the aspect of Vili. According to Norse cosmology, Vili was the brother (or aspect) of Odin who gave to humanity their physical being: flesh, bones, form and function. This represents the purely physical side of humanity, that aspect we share with all lifeforms in one variation or another. For our purposes, this is the Will, the primal instincts and urges that keep us alive and that help propagate the species. Vili finds expression in the first two chakras (three, if you count the navel center), and in the lower tiers of Maslow's hierarchy of needs. These runes are associated with the lower consciousness, with the reptilian brain stem and limbic system, and with physicality.

In *Odin's Lots*, these are represented by the black die with white characters.

Fehu

Sound: <u>F</u>ire
Meaning: Cattle
Level: Physical
Element: Earth
Realm: Niflheim
Image: An ox with upraised horns
Keywords: Wealth, money, resources, support, potential

The first Rune is Fehu, which literally means cattle. It is generally interpreted as wealth since, among the ancient Norse, one's wealth was represented by the number of cattle he owned.

In actuality, cattle on the hoof were not that valuable. Dairy was not widespread at the time and was just coming into use as a food source. Today, after generations of adaptation, many people still have difficulty digesting dairy products. This, we can imagine, was even worse in ancient times when humans first began consuming them.

So, even if you had milk cows, their value was somewhat limited from a nourishment standpoint. The true value was in their meat, in their leather, in their bones and sinew, things that you could only get after you had slaughtered the cow.

While Fehu can mean a direct measurement of wealth or money,

I like to look at it as unmanifest potential. The cow, even money, represents a future promise. Money, in and of itself, does nothing for you unless you spend it to buy food, shelter, clothing, goods and services, etc.

A way to remember the meaning of this rune is by its very shape. You can imagine a cow with its horns upraised into the air. Also, Fehu is directly related to the modern English word fee.

When you see this rune in a runecasting, you can generally apply the interpretation of wealth, of potential. It could also be seen as support, as allies, as encouragement or empowerment to take a certain course of action. Fehu can stand directly for money. It can stand for tools, material resources, even emotional support.

If Fehu is reversed (that is, upside down), we apply the opposite meaning. In this case, it means a lack of those things, or at least a perceived lack of those things on the part of the character. It may suggest a need or craving for money in and of itself, for its own sake. It may suggest a lack of resources, poverty, or monetary loss.

It could also mean the absence of support or encouragement from one's family, one's peer group or tribe.

Uruz

Sound: M<u>oo</u>n
Meaning: Aurochs (European bison)
Level: Physical
Element: Earth
Realm: Asgard
Image: An aurochs preparing to charge
Keywords: Strength, motivation, desire-to-action, procreation

The second rune is Uruz. This literally means the aurochs, the ancient European bison. Though now extinct, the aurochs was huge, larger even than the American bison.

Reports of bison carcasses or preserved remains suggest they may have been seven feet tall at the shoulders, with a seven- or eight-foot horn span. These were terrifying creatures, and very territorial. In tribal societies, for a young man coming into his initiation, his rite of passage into manhood, his task might be to hunt down and kill one of these massive beasts.

In this we find our interpretation of Uruz. Similar to Fehu, or cattle, Uruz suggests potential, but this is potential that is about to release. It is on that cusp of potential energy turning into kinetic energy. The shape of the rune suggests the outline of an aurochs with its horns lowered, preparing to charge. It is that potential on the verge of becoming reality. When we see this in a runecasting, we can interpret it in a number of ways. One general interpretation is power, potency, strength, and virility. This can be procreative virility, or even dominance.

Another interpretation is that some choice or desire is about to turn into action. In the case of the aurochs, this might be the desire to protect its territory manifesting into the action of charging down on that young warrior and turning him into dust. Uruz can also be interpreted as innate sexual drive, that urge to procreate as the aurochs bull is about to chase down its mate.

Reversed, Uruz suggests impotence. This might be either a general powerlessness or physical, sexual impotence. It could indicate a lack of desire, indecisiveness.

If we think of Uruz as indicating potential energy about to become kinetic, the reversal indicates a block of that energy transfer. The character lacks the power and drive to turn the potential of desire into action. This may be due to a lack of agency, absence of will power, or simple uncertainty regarding a course of action.

Thurisaz

Sound: <u>Th</u>orn
Meaning: Giant
Level: Physical
Element: Fire
Realm: Jotunheim
Image: War hammer, thorn
Keywords: Boundaries, defense, organization

The third rune is Thurisaz. In the literal meaning of this word, Thurisaz represents the giants, the thurse beings. These are variously interpreted as ogres, ettins, or Jotnar. These are the inhabitants of Jotunheim, or Giant Home.

In the pre-Grimm mythical world, the giants were not always seen as monsters. Several of the Norse deities were struck speechless by the beauty of certain giants or giantesses. Other giants were endowed with great wisdom. The Jotnar were not always cruel, mindless creatures stomping about the countryside and destroying everything in sight.

A careful examination of the Norse myths suggests the giants were quite literally forces of nature. In one particular mythic episode, Thor—famed for his giant-hunting prowess—enters a wrestling contest with various giants who are the embodiments of old age, fire, the tides, even gravity. Fate itself was represented by the giantesses known as the Norns or the Wyrd Sisters. All these forces are necessary for life, for humanity to exist. Unchecked and unbounded, however, they will destroy us. Mythically, Thor serves as that balance, keeping the titanic powers in check. Thurisaz, then, can be interpreted as balance, as boundaries, as individuality. Its appearance in a runecasting suggests that boundaries are respected, that a person's sense of individuality and their personal boundaries are secure.

When we see this rune reversed, the opposite is true. The character's boundaries are not being respected, either by themselves or others. This may be expressed as someone who is always being trampled on, who is in a codependent or toxic relationship, or who is suffering outright abuse. Thurisaz reversed may also suggest that your character is not respecting the boundaries of others.

Ansuz

Sound:	<u>A</u>hh
Meaning:	Deity
Level:	Physical
Element:	Earth
Realm:	Svartalfheim
Image:	Odin's cloak and beard billowing in the wind
Keywords:	Inspiration, guidance, communication

The fourth rune is Ansuz. The word means deity, specifically one of the Ás or Os. These were the early names of what we now call the Aesir, the gods of Asgard. Other Germanic languages ascribe to Ansuz the meaning of mouth or river. Regardless, the general interpretation of this rune is divine communication or inspiration.

We can see in the rune a representation of Odin, chief of the Aesir, walking hunched over a bit, as in a storm. With a little imagination, we can envision him in his wizard's hat, which he was known to wear in his various guises. We can see his cloak or his beard flowing out behind him. This is one way to visualize and remember this rune.

As the rune of divine communication, of guidance and inspiration, when it appears in a casting, Ansuz means those lines of communication are open. The subject of the runecasting, be it a character or some other story element, is open to the forces of communication in general, of good news. Communication is free-flowing, it is being properly transmitted and received. It may also suggest that the character is offering good advice or is open to and receiving good advice. Reversed, naturally, we have the opposite meaning, which can be taken a couple of ways. The character may be closed off and simply not listening. It could also be that the mentors who would offer their advice are being silenced, either by their own will or from another cause. Ansuz reversed might suggest abandonment, prayers not being heard, even intercepted communications. If you're writing a spy thriller, for example, it could imply a communique gone astray. It could indicate false information, a double agent, or so on.

Raidho

Sound: Ritual
Meaning: Ride
Level: Physical
Element: Earth
Realm: Muspelheim
Image: Horse's hindquarters
Keywords: Right-action, ritual, true path

The fifth rune is Raidho, which means ride. With a little squinting, the shape of the rune suggests the hindquarters of a horse just stepping off. While the meaning can be interpreted as riding a horse, it is more commonly seen as riding on a wagon being pulled by a horse or an ox. This idea of riding on a wagon, as opposed to being in the saddle, is an important one for the interpretation of the rune.

In trying to go from point A to point B, being on foot provides the option of a straight shot cross-country. On horseback, there is similar flexibility, but not quite as much. For example, dense woods can be navigated by infantrymen but present more of a challenge for cavalry. In riding a wagon, there are even more significant challenges in choosing the route. The wagon is limited to a cart path or a road, a way that is well traveled.

This is key to interpreting Raidho. A worn track relies on collective consciousness, on the knowledge and experience of those who have gone that way before. At first glance, roads don't always make sense in their meanderings. With a little examination, however, we discover that they may be avoiding property lines or difficult terrain. They may be longer and more tortuous than the crow's flight, but the traveler will make better time by avoiding all the obstacles. This is the underlying sense of Raidho.

The Indo-European root word associated with Raidho is *rta. This is the root of the English word right, in all its varied meanings and spellings: The right way to go, the right hand, to write with a pen on paper, even the holy rite. All these words stem from the root word, *rta and they share a common basis with the notion of Raidho, which gives a sense of being on the right path.

When Raidho appears in your runecasting, the character or situation is on the right path to go from point A to point B. The character is doing things in the right way. It may imply ritual, which is the formalization of right action. It suggests the idea of things being done properly, of orderliness, of the correct steps being taken.

Conversely, if Raidho appears reversed, there is the notion of being on the wrong path or not staying on the path. There's a sense of shortcuts being taken, of corners being cut, of wrongdoing. These shortcuts may be expedient, they may be profitable, but ultimately, Raidho reversed suggests that things are not being done in the right manner.

Kenaz

Sound:	Keep
Meaning:	Torch
Level:	Physical
Element:	Fire
Realm:	Helheim
Image:	Torch casting a shadow
Keywords:	Knowledge, understanding, creativity, skill

The sixth rune is Kenaz, which means torch. The shape of the rune suggests a torch being stuck into the ground or into a holder and casting its own shadow. It is illuminating itself and also hiding its own light. This notion of light and shadow helps with the interpretation of Kenaz.

Etymologically, Kenaz is related to the English word can, as in, "Can I do this?" While grammar police will often correct this usage ("I don't know. Can you? You may if you like."), the use of *can* is correct in light of the ancient association with Kenaz.

In this sense, *can* has a threefold meaning. Is the character physically capable of doing the thing? Does the character have the right and the moral authority to do it? And does the character possess the skill and mental capacity to do it?

To tie into yet another related word, does the character know (ken) how to do the thing? All three of these aspects come into play when interpreting Kenaz. When it appears in a runecasting, it suggests the idea of knowledge, of knowing how to do something. There is also the idea of understanding, of creativity, of skill. All these combine to suggest that the character can do the thing at hand. Reversed, we see the other side of that coin. It suggests inability. It suggests ignorance. It may also suggest confusion or inappropriateness. There may be knowledge without authority. Perhaps physical ability exists but not the knowledge to achieve something. Kenaz reversed means at least one leg is missing from the three-legged stool of knowledge, physical ability, and moral agency.

Gebo

Sound: Gather
Meaning: Gift
Level: Physical
Element: Æther
Realm: Vanaheim
Image: Hands clasped in greeting
Keywords: Generosity, balance, fair trade

The seventh rune is Gebo. This is a particularly interesting rune with regard to the customs of the ancient Norse people. Gebo means gift, though its shape doesn't necessarily make that connection obvious. On deeper inspection, however, consider the situation of a long-anticipated meeting, either with a stranger or a loved one. Rather than a simple shaking of hands, such greetings might be met with the clasping of both hands. Those clasped hands and forearms form the cross of Gebo to create this X-shape.

This is the power behind Gebo. Hospitality was of great importance among the ancient Norse. The rules of hospitality were not simply courtesies, they were critical to survival among the ancients. The act of bringing someone into the home imposed an unwritten contract upon both host and guest. If a stranger came to the door, the homeowner was obliged to feed and shelter their guest. Conversely, the guest was under strict obligation to act in a peaceful and courteous manner. This notion of giving and receiving, of mutually beneficial behavior, is implicit to Gebo. It is giving and receiving. In its broadest interpretation, it is a fair and equal exchange. Gebo is balance, free flow, cooperation.

Gebo is also the first rune that has no reverse. Geometrically, it is the same right side up or upside down. When it shows up in a runecasting, it has the notion of a universal law that cannot be violated. This is a very benefic rune in that it symbolizes all good things, which cannot be reversed or taken away.

In thrillers or action stories, Gebo can present a challenge to the author. It can seem boring because there's not a negative side to this rune, but this in itself can be an interesting plot point. Within the context of where Gebo appears in the runecasting, of its relation to other runes, or of how it wants to show up in the story, there are certainly ways to take this into account.

Wunjo

Sound: <u>W</u>isdom
Meaning: Joy
Level: Physical
Element: Earth
Realm: Ljossalfheim
Image: Tribal banner
Keywords: Joy, achievement, completion

The eighth rune, last of the first aett, is Wunjo, whose literal meaning is joy. As with Gebo, when this rune appears upright it signifies really good things. The shape of the rune is that of a pennant. In ancient times, this would have been reflected in the shape of a clan or tribal banner that might fly over the camp, a guidepost for people to find their way. Alternately, if it were the banner of a rival or hostile tribe, it provided fair warning to keep your distance.

In the context of this first aett, especially as discussed with Uruz and the young hunter's initiation, Wunjo's meaning becomes clear. Our young warrior has gone out on his initiatory hunt. He has overcome the hardships and dangers to bring down his first kill, the wild aurochs. In addition to proving his worth and skill as a hunter-warrior, he has obtained valuable resources for his tribe.

Now, as he nears his homeland, he sees a banner. Perhaps the wind is low or it's in the wrong direction. He sees the banner but can't quite make it out. Then the wind changes. The banner snaps up and the young hunter sees that it's his tribe, his clan. He has come home. This is the joy that Wunjo implies. Beyond simply the joy of the return home is the sense of achievement. The hunter-initiate left as a boy. He has experienced untold trials, fears, doubts. He's overcome all of these, achieved his objective, and returned to claim his new position and to share his bounty with the tribe.

In the Hero's Journey cycle, which we'll examine further in the Nine Worlds runecasting, Wunjo fills a very important role. It represents the Return, the completion of the journey. The character has ventured into the Extraordinary World, the magical land of the story. Our hero has faced the demons, achieved the boon, then returned to the Ordinary World. Wunjo is this joy, this sense of homecoming, of a completed journey. It gives a sense of achievement, a job well done, and the joy that comes from this.

Reversed, we have the opposite of these things. Opposite of joy could be depression, perhaps indifference. There may be a sense of neglect in that someone is not doing what they ought to. They're not fulfilling their duties and their obligations.

Alternately, this might show up as a sense of ingratitude. The character has gone out and completed this arduous task, achieved the goal, and brought the boon back home. Our hero returns to the village, and the tribe reacts with indifference, perhaps even scorn. What should be a sense of pride on the character's part goes unappreciated. There's no joy when they come home.

Wunjo reversed could also represent the failed Hero's Journey. The character may refuse to return to the Ordinary World or, returning, may refuse to share the boon with the tribe. We get a sense of this from Tolkien. Though we don't know exactly what occurred between *There and Back Again* and *The Lord of the Rings*, we can infer a failed Hero's Journey. Bilbo has developed a certain madness. He's completed his journey, found his treasure, but he's held on to it for himself, unwilling to share the boon with the shire.

This is the tragic Hero's Journey. Bilbo returned home changed—as all heroes do—but not necessarily for the better. He's unwilling or unable to allow the community to benefit from his change. Maybe there is no benefit, and that's part of the tragedy of the story. This is the sense of Wunjo reversed. He's come home but he really hasn't. There's no joy in the homecoming. There's no fulfillment for the journeyer or the village in this return.

Wunjo reversed is perhaps the most tragic rune. Where there should be great joy, great achievement, instead we have loss, sorrow, neglect. Instead of victory and joy, ungratefulness or disdain welcomes the hero home.

The Second Aett

THE SECOND AETT IS ASSOCIATED with the aspect of Ve.
According to Norse cosmology, Ve was the brother (or aspect)
of Odin who gave to humanity their mental and emotional being:
heart, blood, the ability to feel. This represents the intellectual and
emotional side of humanity, that aspect we share with mammals and
other higher lifeforms.

For our purposes, this is the Ordinary Consciousness, the part
of the mind that enables us to navigate physical reality and interact
with others and the world around us. Ve finds expression in the
middle three chakras, and in the central tiers of Maslow's hierarchy
of needs. These runes are associated with waking consciousness,
with the cerebral cortex, and with mental and emotional functions.

In Odin's Lots, these are represented by the red die with black
characters.

Hagalaz

Sound: H̲eavy
Meaning: Hail
Level: Psychological
Element: Water
Realm: Niflheim
Image: Bridging of Mist-Home and Fire-Home
Keywords: Cleansing, purification

The ninth rune, first of the second aett, is Hagalaz. The word means hail, as in the balls of ice that fall from the sky. To find a mnemonic for the shape of this rune, we turn to ancient Norse cosmology.

At the beginning of the manifest universe was Ginungagap (Yawning Chasm), the primordial void. Shortly following (or, perhaps, coincident with) the Big Bang, the first two realms of Yggdrasil, the World Tree, emerged. These were Muspelheim (Fire Home) and Niflheim (Mist or Water Home).

Fire from Muspelheim leapt across the void, contacted the ice of Niflheim, and began melting it, evaporating it. The steam that rose from the ice then condensed, refroze, and fell as hail. That hail was absorbed back into the ice, only to be heated up again by the fire of Muspelheim. This alchemical process of repeated evaporation and condensation resulted in a brine, out of which arose the first primordial life. This first being, Ymir, became the father of the giants, great-grandfather of Odin, and the foundation of Midgard, our Earth. This is how we can remember the shape of Hagalaz. Muspelheim stands on one side of Ginungagap, Niflheim on the other, with a bridge across the void.

When Hagalaz appears in a reading, it is typically interpreted as some sort of purification. The shape cannot be reversed, but most contemporary rune readers will view this as a negative or malefic rune. I take some exception to this stance.

While Hagalaz literally means hail, it can stand in for rain, drizzle, snow, etc. Just as precipitation can take many forms, so too with purification. It may come as a gentle snowfall, blanketing the earth in purest white. It may form a drizzle or a steady rain that slowly clears the streets of debris. Or it may come as a flash flood or hail storm that flattens everything in its path.

Your story and your character's journey will dictate how this purification comes into play. How the purification is received will impact its dramatic import to your story. If the character recognizes and accepts the need for change, the purification comes as a warm bath where she rinses off the old, towels off, and is ready for something new. It could be as gentle and subtle as that. If she's grasping and clinging to certain aspects of her story, it may take the force of a hailstorm to knock off the detritus, to beat her down until all that's left is her core essence.

Nauthiz

Sound: <u>N</u>ormal
Meaning: Need
Level: Psychological
Element: Water
Realm: Asgard
Image: Bow drill for fire-starting
Keywords: Necessity, emergency, innovation

The tenth rune, second of the second aett, is Nauthiz, which means need or emergency. As with Hagalaz, contemporary rune readers typically (and understandably) interpret this as a negative rune. They view Nauthiz as indicating dire circumstances, some emergency on the horizon. While this may well be an appropriate interpretation, I prefer to view this as the necessity that is the mother of invention. This is the stepping-off point for innovation.

The shape of the rune suggests a bow drill, stave and bow crossed and ready to generate the frictional heat for a fire. For the ancients, the need for fire was a fact of daily existence. The innovation of the bow drill may well be one of the pivotal inventions of human history, which grew out of this existential need.

Imagine being the one to make this leap of innovation, alone and cold in the wilderness with only the occasional lightning strike to make fire for you. You might stumble across the remains of a recent fire, or perhaps someone has carefully carried some embers with them from another village. But these chance occurrences may be as rare and random as a lightning strike.

Now, imagine the level of desperation. You need fire for warmth, to purify your water, to cook your food. Imagine the trial and error, the frustration, and the hopelessness needed to reach the point where rubbing a couple of sticks together seems like a good idea.

This is Nauthiz.

It sits along a spectrum from need, to innovation, to need met. It falls to you and the needs of the story to interpret the manner of the need and of its resolution (or lack thereof). Nauthiz simply requires that something impose a need upon your characters, which may or may not result in something new. That need may persist, where it creates a failure, a gap. Or it may spark something new, some innovation in your story or a new outlook for your character to address that need.

I

Isa

Sound: S<u>ee</u>d
Meaning: Ice
Level: Psychological
Element: Æther
Realm: Jotunheim
Image: Icicle
Keywords: Individuality, integrity

The eleventh rune, third of the second aett, is Isa. Isa literally means ice, and the shape of this rune suggests an icicle.

As with Hagalaz and Nauthiz, Isa is often viewed as a negative rune. The traditional reading suggests a dead stop. Everything has or needs to come to a frozen standstill.

Isa is also frequently interpreted as the ego unchecked. This is a valid interpretation, but the view of ego needn't be a negative one. Yes, there is individuality, there is a separation, and this is a good thing.

I tend to think of this as looking at a roof that has been covered with snow. The sun comes out for a few hours and begins to heat it up. The snow starts to melt and water drips off. But as soon as the water runs into shade, or when the sun goes down, it again begins to freeze.

Soon out of this indistinguishable mass of snow, you have this individualized, individuated icicle. This is the true essence of humanity, of individualization. We have a common basis, we spring from a common well. However, in order to experience the fullness of human existence, we must individuate into a distinct personality within a separate physical body.

It's in this sense that Isa stands for individuation or integrity. This integrity may be in the sense of being righteous and moral and just, but also in the sense of being whole. Mathematically, there are the whole numbers: 1, 2, 3, and so on. These are integral numbers. They are complete in themselves. They are not decimals, not blending into the numbers around them.

In a runecasting, Isa suggests the character is fully individualized and standing within her integrity. It could also suggest isolation or separation. Though Isa cannot be reversed, there is a duality of interpretation, giving the storyteller some flexibility in how to apply it.

Jera

Sound: <u>Y</u>esterday
Meaning: Year
Level: Psychological
Element: Water
Realm: Svartalfheim
Image: Sickle scything into a stalk of grain
Keywords: Harvest, full cycle, patience

The twelfth rune, fourth of the second aett, is Jera. In contradiction to the preceding three runes, Jera is almost universally seen as positive, similar in nature to Gebo. Jera literally means year and has a very similar pronunciation. This is, in fact, the root of the modern English word.

While the entire solar year is suggested by Jera, most interpretations view Jera as relating specifically to the harvest. Graphically, the shape of the rune suggests a sickle scything through a stalk of wheat.

In ancient (and even modern) agrarian societies, the harvest time of late summer or early autumn brought with it a time of celebration. There's a sense of completion, of fulfillment. There is the assurance that the harvest has come in and will see the people through the approaching winter into the spring, into the new hope that lies ahead.

While Wunjo carries a sense of completion and Gebo suggests a gift, Jera has an implied sense of patience. In the springtime was the sowing, and now has come the harvest. But in between was a period of maturation and of growth during which there was not much to do. The seeds were planted then left alone for the earth to bring the crops into fruition, into fulfillment.

With Jera, there is a sense of a long wait being over, that harvest time has come. It also suggests a degree of cooperation. The farmers have done their part by sowing the seeds, then the earth and fertility gods did their part in turning those seeds into crops. Now, the farmers go back out to bring in the harvest.

While Jera is generally seen as quite positive, it could also suggest that trying times lie ahead, that winter is coming. The natural cycle is also suggestive of a gear, another word related to Jera. The wheel of the year and the wheel of fate are closely related. While the harvest is being brought in there is preparation for the coming winter, an eye toward storing some of the seed for the next spring.

Jera suggests this cyclical process that continues on and on. Right now, let's enjoy the reaping. Let's make our harvest beer, set up our mead, and make the first pressing of the grapes. A tough winter may be in store, but now is the time for celebration.

∫

Eihwaz

Sound: ü, French u
Meaning: Yew tree
Level: Psychological
Element: Water
Realm: Muspelheim
Image: Branching yew tree
Keywords: Transformation, death-and-rebirth

The thirteenth rune, fifth of the second aett, is Eihwaz (pronounced Yew-waz), which literally means the yew tree. The shape of the rune is suggestive of this tree, which—in addition to its broad canopy—is known to sprout shoots from the base of the trunk.

As with Hagalaz, Nauthiz, and Isa, Eihwaz is almost universally viewed as a malefic rune, perhaps the most challenging of all. The general interpretation for Eihwaz is transformation, usually of the involuntary sort. This rune is not reversible, and hints that whatever transformation is lined up, there's no avoiding it.

In story terms, this transformation may indicate a major shift in the character's outlook. It might suggest a status change (positive or negative), or perhaps a shift in goals or story objective. In extreme cases it may suggest the ultimate transformation of death and rebirth.

As with Hagalaz, which indicates purification, the transformation suggested by Eihwaz may be welcome or not. It can be graciously received or not. But the fact of the matter is that transformation is coming, one way or another. As with all the so-called challenging runes, Eihwaz presents a great opportunity for character development. After all, character is best revealed through crisis points, and the transformation wrought by Eihwaz is perhaps the most critical among all the runes. How this crisis unfolds and how your character responds to the crisis—how she resists or embraces it—provide great story fodder.

Perthro

Sound:	<u>P</u>ot
Meaning:	Lot cup
Level:	Psychological
Element:	Fire
Realm:	Helheim
Image:	Lot/dice cup on its side
Keywords:	Fortune, fate, chance, randomness, orlog/dharma

The fourteenth rune, sixth of the second aett, is Perthro, which means a lot cup or a dice cup. This meaning is hinted at in the shape of this rune, a stylized dice cup on its side having just cast the lots or dice.

The ancient Norse were inveterate gamblers. Tacitus in his *Germania* tells of the passion that the Germanic tribesmen had for gambling. So great was their love of sport that they would, if they'd lost everything else—their money, their clothing, their farms, and so on—they would wager their own freedom. They were willing to enslave themselves for one last bet.

That's the impression we get from Perthro, but in a deeper sense. There may be a suggestion of randomness or chance, but there's a greater notion of fortune, of fate. This leads us to the Norse idea and ideal of orlog.

Orlog is more than simply fate or chance, more than random circumstance. Its closest cousin would be in the Vedic or East Indian notion of dharma, which connotes one's life purpose.

Perthro suggests that everything is going your character's way. She's on a lucky streak at the table, her number is always coming up (in a good way). She's dialed in to her life purpose and everything is lined up to help her achieve her objective.

Perthro reversed? Not so good.

Reversed, we have bad luck, ill fortune. At a deeper level, there's a sense of karma as opposed to dharma. Whatever the situation or story moment, your character's orlog (at least in that instance) has been achieved and it's time to break with all the things that were supporting it. No matter how hard she tries, nothing is going to bring it back.

If it's a relationship? Over. A job? Done. Like the Tarot's Wheel of Fortune, Perthro—depending on its orientation—can either speed your character to her destiny or steamroller the things that no longer serve her.

Elhaz

Sound:	<u>Z</u>ebra
Meaning:	Elk
Level:	Psychological
Element:	Air
Realm:	Vanaheim
Image:	Elk's antlers
Keywords:	Protection, shaman, mentor, attunement

The fifteenth rune, seventh of the second aett, is Elhaz, which means elk. The European elk with which the Norse would have been familiar was more akin to the North American moose than what we might generally think of as elk. The shape of Elhaz suggests this, with the broad antlers stretching out.

The sense of this rune is one of protection. The European elk, as with North American moose, have huge antlers. While the elk are not particularly territorial, they are quite protective of their young. It's not unknown for an elk or moose to take down a predator if it is threatening their offspring. Either with antlers or hooves, they've been known to kill wolves, even bears.

A subtler interpretation of this rune—in relation to ancient Norse culture—is as a representation of the shaman. Again, we can see this reflected in the shape of the rune: the shaman holds his arms out wide, standing between the gods or the forces of nature and the tribe. There is still the sense of protection, now personified in the shaman. In this sense, Elhaz might also represent a mentor for your character.

Reversed, we have the opposite of this. If upright suggests protection, the reversal may be seen as vulnerability, as weakness, as openness to attack. The means that your character had to protect her—the walls, the shelter, or the protective person standing between her and danger—are gone. There's the sense of impending attack or invasion.

There may also be a suggestion of abandonment, that those who were there to protect her are gone. Or worse, those who stood in a position of protection have turned against her. In both divination and storytelling terms, this can be a really powerful rune.

Sowilo

Sound:	Source
Meaning:	Sun, Soul
Level:	Psychological
Element:	Water
Realm:	Ljossalfheim
Image:	Lightning bolt, rays of the sun
Keywords:	Energy, soul, motivation, success, optimism

The sixteenth rune, last of the second aett, is Sowilo, which literally means Sun. The shape of this rune suggests a ray of sunlight or a bolt of lightning.

In the ancient Germanic languages, the root word of Sowilo is shared with both the word for the Sun (Sol, as in Solar system) and soul (Sawul), that innermost part of our being. The sun was seen by the ancients as the soul or center of our planetary system.

We tend to think that the ancients thought of the Earth as the center of the universe, that everything else revolved around us. However, the very name and the correlation of the Sun with the soul suggests the ancients understood that Earth and the other planets actually do revolve around the Sun.

Sowilo can also be seen as energy, the energy the sun releases in the form of light and heat, which makes life possible on Earth. This interpretation gives the notion of success, of motivation. When the sun comes up in the morning, or the first warm day of spring comes after a cold winter, there's a sense of empowerment, of activation. We're motivated to harness that energy, to make things happen.

Sowilo cannot be reversed and makes it, along with Gebo and Dagaz, one of the most benefic among the runes.

The Third Aett

T HE THIRD AND FINAL AETT IS associated with the highest aspect of Odin.

According to Norse cosmology, Odin gave to humanity the breath of life—literally, inspiration. This represents the spiritual side of humanity, the aspect that uniquely defines us as *homo sapiens sapiens*, the humans who know that they know.

For our purposes, this is the Spirit, the nature that makes us stare up at the night sky with wonder. Odin finds expression in the highest two chakras (three, if you count the *lalana* chakra at the roof of the mouth), and in the upper tiers of Maslow's hierarchy of needs. These runes are associated with the higher consciousness, with the neocortex, with spirituality and higher ideals.

In Odin's Lots, these are represented by the white die with red characters.

Tiwaz

Sound: <u>T</u>uesday
Meaning: The god Tyr/Tiw
Level: Spiritual
Element: Air
Realm: Niflheim
Image: Spear point, or canopy of the sky
Keywords: Honor, self-sacrifice, ordered conduct, directness

The seventeenth rune, first of the third aett, is Tiwaz. This is the ancient name of the god Tiw or Tyr, from which we get Tuesday (Tiw's Day). We can see in the shape of the rune a spearhead or, perhaps more appropriately, a tent pole supporting the canopy of the heavens.

Among the Germanic tribes—in fact among ancient Indo-Europeans as a whole—the earliest god-form of a male deity was the Sky Father. We can recognize this name in the Greek Deus/Theus/Zeus, the Roman Dyeus (from which we derive Jupiter, or Dyeus Pater). Even among the ancient (non-Indo-European) Chinese, the sky god was called Di or Ti. All of these share the same root with Tiwaz.

One of the most popular myths related to Tyr is a tale of the wolf Fenrir, one of the offspring of the mischief-maker Loki. When Fenrir was a puppy, the gods loved to play with him. As he began to grow, however, his appetite was unbounded and the gods feared he would eventually consume the entire world. The Aesir decided to bind Fenrir, but no rope or chain could stand up to him. The gods then went to the Dwarfs, the magical artisans, and charged them to craft an unbreakable binding. The result was Gleipnir, a silk-like ribbon made of pure subtlety.

The Aesir summoned Fenrir and told him that if he wanted to achieve great fame (the desire for which was the cause of his insatiable hunger), he must break free of Gleipnir. Now, he'd already broken a thick rope and a massive chain. To snap a thin ribbon was nothing. Sensing treachery, Fenrir agreed to the test, but only if one of the Aesir agreed to place his hand in the wolf's mouth as surety against any tricks. After much bickering, Tyr finally stepped forward to meet Fenrir's demand. Sure enough, the binding held and Tyr, defender of Asgard, lost his sword hand.

This myth gives us the symbolic meaning of Tiwaz. We see forthrightness, an aversion to subtlety. It suggests there is a job to be done, and the character will do it regardless of the personal cost. Tiwaz stands for honor, strength, fortitude, and directness.

Reversed, we have the opposite of these traits. We see subtlety and cleverness. It might suggest spy-craft or intrigue, perhaps a heist caper that is just a bit too clever. These things are anathema to the warrior ethos. Where the warrior is forthright, Tiwaz reversed suggests more of a spy mentality.

Berkano

Sound: <u>B</u>erry
Meaning: Birch
Level: Spiritual
Element: Fire
Realm: Asgard
Image: Twin-lobed birch seed; a mother's breasts
Keywords: Nourishment, care-giving, new life, endurance

The eighteenth rune, second of the third aett, is Berkano. Berkano means the birch tree, and its shape reflects the twin lobes of the birch seed. The shape is also suggestive of a mother's breasts, which ties in with the rune's interpretation.

The birch tree is considered a pioneer species. In the aftermath of a cataclysmic event such as a forest fire, a great flood, or—in the case of the ancient Norse—glacial retreat, when all plant life has been wiped out, the birch tree is one of the first plants to take hold. Able to grow in harsh environments, the birch takes root and stabilizes the soil. After several seasons, its dropped leaves decay and fertilize the ground, allowing more plant types to grow and animals to forage. Over time, the biodiversity of the formerly barren land is restored, thanks to the powerful birch.

This gives us the sense of Berkano, which stands for nourishment, growth, motherhood, and new life. Berkano in a runecasting suggests hope, nurturing, health, and physical and emotional wellbeing. Reversed, of course, suggests the opposite. There is sickness. There is neglect. There is perhaps emotional distance, the idea that the caretaker, the nourisher has turned her back on her child. As applies to your story, this could represent a bad mother, either the character or the character's mother-figure. As with Ansuz and Elhaz, Berkano reversed can be devastating in terms of the story. These runes of power and support and protection, when reversed, suggest great tragedy.

Ehwaz

Sound: Pl<u>ea</u>sure
Meaning: Horse
Level: Spiritual
Element: Air
Realm: Jotunheim
Image: Horse's head; bridle and reins
Keywords: Intuition, innate knowledge, trust, instinct, gut feeling

The nineteenth rune, third of the third aett, is Ehwaz, which means horse. We see in the name of this rune a close cousin to the Latin *equus*, and its shape suggests a horse's head or reins and a bridle.

In a runecasting, Ehwaz denotes intuition, innate knowledge, and instinct. These meanings stem from the connection between horse and rider. Consider the intuitive connection between an experienced rider and a well-trained horse. The rider can seemingly will the horse's movements with his mind without touching the reins. There may be subtle physical cues unconsciously communicated between rider and horse, but the depth of connection—if not its exact nature—is indisputable.

Ehwaz also represents the trust between horse and rider. When well paired and well matched, each has trust in the other for their experience, their ability, and their knowledge of where they're going. Whereas with Raidho, the ride, the sense is more about being on the right path, with Ehwaz the sense is more about following a true path. It may not be a well-traveled path, but it is a sure path for this horse-and-rider pairing.

Reversed, we have the opposite: mistrust, the betrayal of trust, doubting one's gut feelings. The character may act contrary to what she knows is the best course of action, either because everyone else is going that way or because she has failed in some way and no longer trusts her intuition. In this sense, Ehwaz reversed suggests more of a self-betrayal than betrayal by another person in that position of trust. This is very much an internal rune. If there is a conflict, it's generally going to be an inner conflict between the character and her own knowledge or instinct.

Mannaz

Sound: <u>M</u>oon
Meaning: Human, Mind, Moon
Level: Spiritual
Element: Air
Realm: Svartalfheim
Image: Reflection; Union of two equals
Keywords: Unity, cooperation, mind, meditation

The twentieth rune, fourth of the third aett, is Mannaz. Mannaz means man and connotes a human being, not specifically a male. The shape of the rune is suggestive of this. Where Wunjo's symbol represents a tribal flag or clan banner, Mannaz represents the meeting of two banners, one as the reflection of the other. This suggests a transcendence of clan, tribe, or nation and points to our shared humanity, the reflection of the one in the other.

Mannaz also shares a root with the words for moon and mind. There's a direct correlation here with Sowilo (sun, soul). Just as the moon's light is really a reflection of the sun, so the brilliance of the mind is but the reflection of the soul. This offers a deep lesson, both in life and in character development. Human beings are soul creatures inhabiting a body, with the mind as the intermediary between those two aspects. In the same way, the moon functions as something of an intermediary between Sun and Earth.

If someone stares into the sun, he may go blind and handicap himself in his navigation of the physical environment. In a similar manner, if we focus too heavily on the soul, we may miss out on this earthly experience, which is the whole point of incarnating into a physical body. By contrast, even under the brightest full moon, our heaven-gazer can stare into the moon and do no damage. Similarly, we can marvel on the mind and still be able to go about our physical existence.

With regard to character-development, the soul of a person (real or fictitious) is very difficult to glimpse and all but impossible to describe in dynamic narrative. In contrast, the mind—by its projections through word, thought, and action—offers a reflection of the soul, the true essence of the character. When Mannaz appears in a runecasting, it denotes a sound mind, mental stability, and a sense of shared humanity.

Reversed, we get the notion of mental upset, perhaps even mental illness or instability. It may also suggest a sense of isolation, of clannishness or tribalism, where the character can no longer see himself reflected in the Other. Anytime we see a failure to recognize the commonality and shared value of human experience, that is indicative of Mannaz reversed.

ᛚ

Laguz

Sound: Lagoon
Meaning: Lake
Level: Spiritual
Element: Earth
Realm: Muspelheim
Image: Wave crest; fishing gaffe
Keywords: Emotions, personal connection, life-force energy

The twenty-first rune, fifth of the third aett, is Laguz. It literally means lake or water, and we can see in its shape a wave crest, or perhaps a fishing gaffe. As water is almost universally considered symbolic of emotion, Laguz gives us a sense of those still waters that run deep.

The Germanic people, as forerunners of the great Norse and Norman navigators, knew all about the power of the seas. Being more suggestive of inland waters, Laguz begins to provide its own meaning. The waters of a lake can be explored. They can be circumnavigated, you can know all the terrain around the lake. You may not be able to plumb its depths, depending on how deep it is, but you can know all of the terrain surrounding it. This in contradistinction to the open sea whose bounds—in ancient times, at least—could never be fully explored.

With Laguz, then, we have a sense of certainty and safety in navigating the emotional waters. There may be ups and downs, we may never truly know their depths, but we can understand the environment surrounding them. The shore is always in sight.

Reversed, Laguz suggests emotional turmoil. This is not simply the experience of so-called negative emotions. Sadness or anger can be as powerful agents for change as satisfaction or joy—perhaps even more so. No, the truly dangerous emotional waters are those that are muddied. They may hide sandbars, rocks, or shoals that can tear the belly out of a ship. Laguz reversed indicates a disconnect from one's emotions or their suppression to the point that a violent storm is moments away, and no one will see it coming.

Ingwaz

Sound: Si**ng**
Meaning: The god Yngvi/Ingunar-Frey
Level: Spiritual
Element: Æther
Realm: Helheim
Image: Seed; spark or burning ember
Keywords: Inspiration, inner drive, incubation

The twenty-second rune, sixth of the third aett, is Ingwaz. Its literal meaning is the name of the god Ingwaz—later identified as Ingunar or Yngvi. This deity is generally considered equivalent to the better-known Frey, one of the Vanir who resided among the Aesir as part of the peace treaty between the two races of gods. (More about this in the section on the Nine Worlds in Part Three.)

Frey was a fertility god and an ancestor deity. We see in the shape of this rune the seed that may bring forth new life, or the spark (or flame-seed) that may create new fire. This relation between Frey, fire, and the ancestors is celebrated even today in the inglenook, the corner hearth that warms many homes and provides a place to honor family and the ancestors.

Ingwaz, then, suggests inspiration, incubation, an inner drive. We get a sense of this hidden spark coming forth, bursting into life. As with the seed, there is the idea of life growing within a shell until it can no longer be contained and it bursts into external life. Or it may be the ember that glows and is fed until it erupts into flame.

In terms of runecasting, Ingwaz may suggest an idea whose time has come, a re-emergence after a time in hiding, perhaps even an unexpected pregnancy. Anything that relates to a period of silence, darkness, or secrecy followed by an obvious and irrevocable emergence into the world is fair game for this rune.

Ingwaz cannot be reversed. While it is generally interpreted in a positive light, the implications of a long-planted seed finally bearing fruit may have positive or negative implications for your story world.

Dagaz

Sound:	<u>D</u>ig, <u>Th</u>ere
Meaning:	Day
Level:	Spiritual
Element:	Æther
Realm:	Vanaheim
Image:	Sunrise/sunset
Keywords:	Cycle, awakening, fun, blessing, reward

The twenty-third rune, seventh of the third aett, is Dagaz, which means day. The shape is commonly seen in the design of shutters on European homes, a subtle link to the daylight they admit or block. The shape of Dagaz also calls to mind the idea of sunrise or sunset, the balance of daylight hours.

Through this imagery we find the general interpretation of Dagaz as a short cycle (as opposed to the longer span of Jera). If we consider the rune to indicate sunrise, there is a sense of awakening, of a new dawn. On the other side, with sunset, Dagaz hints at achievement, accomplishment, reward.

Consider the original meaning of this. Our ancient Norseman has been out hunting or working in the fields or tending the nets by day. Now the sun is sinking toward the horizon. The day is coming to an end and it's time to go home to his family. There awaits the hearth, fire and warmth and food. There awaits good cheer and rest, the reward for his day's labor.

As with Gebo and Jera, Dagaz is a very beneficent rune and cannot be reversed.

Othala

Sound:	B<u>oa</u>t
Meaning:	Inheritance
Level:	Spiritual
Element:	Air
Realm:	Ljossalfheim
Image:	Homestead; house framing
Keywords:	Home, family, security, continuity

The twenty-fourth and final rune, eighth of the third aett, is Othala. Othala literally means inheritance, and in its shape we can make out the timber framing and rafters of an old family homestead, the great hall.

With this meaning of inheritance (sometimes seen as heritage), there is the sense of home and family, of security and continuity. Unlike Wunjo and Dagaz, which carry with them some notion of merit, of reward for one's efforts, the inheritance of Othala is far easier to obtain. One needn't necessarily work for an inheritance, he may not need to accomplish anything to be included in the will. He simply needs to keep his nose clean, remain in reasonably good standing, and not tick anyone off too badly. Within these modest guidelines, the inheritance is almost assured.

When I was young, my mother's family held a reunion each year with upward of two hundred people and five generations of aunts, uncles, and cousins many times removed. The get-together was held at the old homestead where my grandfather and his eleven siblings were raised. I can still recall the rolling hills of Ohio and the sense of excitement upon cresting the last hill when the farmhouse came into view. There was family. There were close cousins I hadn't seen in a year, but with whom we could pick right up where we'd last left off. There were grand stories—most threadbare, but some new. There was history. There was family.

This is the sense of Othala.

Reversed, of course, we find the opposite. We're faced with exile, abandonment, rejection—either by the family against the individual, or by the individual choosing to seek her own path. Othala may also suggest homelessness, poverty, the sense of being bereft of choices and at the end of one's rope. Whether by choice, by poor behavior, or by familial shenanigans, the character has been cut off, cast adrift, and left to her own devices.

The Journey Back

Runecasting

T HE FOLLOWING RUNECASTINGS may be done with cards, tiles, stones, or whatever style of runestaves you please. The first runecasting is intended specifically for Odin's Lots, but may be adapted to other rune styles or standard six-sided dice.

When using rune cards, it is important to shuffle the deck completely, randomizing both order and orientation. Overhand or riffle shuffles are fine, so long as the cards can be sufficiently randomized without bending or scoring. Three to five shuffles will fully randomize the deck.

If a card slips out or appears face-up during the shuffle, it should be placed in the spread in the order and orientation in which it appears. This generally implies a strong subconscious hit, akin to the Muse hitting you over the head.

Referring to the following layouts, place the cards face-up in the numerical sequence shown. Each card position represents a specific story or character element, as described below.

The runecastings presented here are specific to story, plot, and character development. With practice, you should feel free to modify the layouts and interpretations as you see fit.

There is no one, right way to interpret any given card or casting. As with writing itself, the joy (and the challenge) of runecasting is in the process and in the discovery. In any given reading, if a particular rune doesn't feel right or you can't fathom its meaning, feel free to pick a new card or exchange its position with another card in the casting.

For each runecasting I present a sample layout and interpretation, based on a specific story idea I had in mind. I won't go deep into the meaning of each rune, just its interpretation in the context of that particular runecasting and story. If you've jumped ahead, you may want to go back to Part Two for a deeper dive into the meaning and interpretation of each Rune.

Storytelling is a creative, intuitive process. There are no hard and fast rules. As such, you (and your Muse) have complete control. The Runes are here to serve your story, to make the process easier, not harder. Use the Runes and these castings as best fits your nature and your story.

Above all, enjoy!

Odin's Lots

IN NORSE MYTHOLOGY, THE CHIEF god Odin is said to have two brothers, Ve and Vili (sometimes called Honir and Lod). These three individuals can be interpreted as a threefold nature, the Norse trinity.

The Eddic poem *Voluspa* (*The Seeress's Prophecy*) includes an account of the creation of the physical world. According to the poem, after the brothers created Midgard (Earth) from the body of the primordial giant Ymir, they stumbled upon two creatures, Ask and Embla. To these Odin gave breath, Ve gave senses, and Vili gave hair. In this manner, the trinity can be associated with the three aspects of humanity: body (Vili), mind (Ve), and spirit (Odin). Alternately, from a psychological perspective, these may represent the lower consciousness, ordinary consciousness, and higher consciousness.

The Odin's Lots runecasting applies this threefold nature to character development. Each eight-sided die contains the runes of one of the three aetts and is associated with one of the Odinic aspects. This casting is intended to be used in the preliminary stages of characterization, defining the character's inner conflict, and should not fundamentally change during the story.

Focus on the character in question. Shake and roll the dice. The reading may be interpreted as follows.

(1) VILI - THE WOUND

The first aett of Vili relates to the character's Wound. This represents some trauma or tragedy experienced by the character—usually in childhood—that has shaped her view of the world and the way she responds to it. The character may be unaware of the wound or, if aware, she mistakenly believes she has dealt with and overcome it. The rune for this position is generally interpreted as being reversed (with the exception of Gebo, which cannot be reversed).

(2) VE - THE IDENTITY

The second aett of Ve signifies the character's Identity. This is who we meet at the beginning of the story, the persona or mask the character has put on—consciously or unconsciously—to enable her to cope with her wound and navigate the world around her. Living within her identity keeps the character safe, but unfulfilled. As Michael Hauge of *Story Mastery* explains it, the story the character tells herself in adopting this identity is always logical, and always a lie. This rune may be interpreted as upright or reversed.

(3) ODIN - THE ESSENCE

The third aett of Odin stands for the character's Essence. This is the best and highest aspect of who she truly is. This nature is in direct conflict with the Identity, and completes the setup for her inner struggle. As she moves through the story, this is the person she must become in order to achieve her outer goal, her inner need, or both. This rune will generally be read upright, but could be interpreted as reversed.

Alternate Methods

If you do not have a set of Odin's Lots, this runecasting may be made using cards, tiles, or standard dice.

If using cards or tiles, separate them into the three aetts. Shuffle and turn up a card or tile from each set independently, and interpret as described above.

For standard dice, roll two dice for each aett. If rolled at once, each pair of dice should have a distinct color or pattern. Alternately, roll for each aett separately.

Roll	1	2	3	4	5	6
1		ᚠ·ᚺ·↑	ᚠ·ᚺ·↑	ᚢ·ᛏ·ᛒ	ᚦ·ᛁ·ᛗ	
2	ᚠ·ᚺ·↑	ᛈ·ᛋ·ᛉ	ᚢ·ᛏ·ᛒ	ᚦ·ᛁ·ᛗ	ᚠ·ᛞ·ᛗ	ᚱ·ᛊ·ᚲ
3	ᚠ·ᚺ·↑	ᚢ·ᛏ·ᛒ	ᛈ·ᛋ·ᛉ	ᚠ·ᛞ·ᛗ	ᚱ·ᛊ·ᚲ	<·ᛖ·◇
4	ᚢ·ᛏ·ᛒ	ᚦ·ᛁ·ᛗ	ᚠ·ᛞ·ᛗ	ᛈ·ᛋ·ᛉ	<·ᛖ·◇	X·ᛦ·⋈
5	ᚦ·ᛁ·ᛗ	ᚠ·ᛞ·ᛗ	ᚱ·ᛊ·ᚲ	<·ᛖ·◇	ᛈ·ᛋ·ᛉ	X·ᛦ·⋈
6		ᚱ·ᛊ·ᚲ	<·ᛖ·◇	X·ᛦ·⋈	X·ᛦ·⋈	

If the dice come up 1+1, 1+6, or 6+6, these combinations are void and the dice should be rolled again. Rolls totaling 3 or 4 (excluding double-2) indicate the first rune of the aett. Rolls totaling 5 through 9 (excluding doubles) indicate the second through sixth runes, respectively. A roll summing up to 10 or 11 (excluding double-5) points to the seventh rune. Finally, a roll of doubles (excluding 1+1 and 6+6) results in the eighth rune.

Further Options

The use of Odin's Lots is not limited to character development. Any threefold story challenge may be tackled by using this roll of the dice.

Examples include Goal-Motivation-Conflict, Past-Present-Future, a threefold choice (such as Lover A, Lover B, or going it alone), and so on.

Feel free to experiment with different story challenges. Share your personal favorites and outcomes at www.runesforwriters.com or on the *Runes for Writers* Facebook page.

Sample Runecasting

For this runecasting, I used the *Odin's Lots* dice sets and a wooden dice cup (literally, a perthro). The lots came up as Kenaz, Eihwaz, and Laguz.

Kenaz represents knowledge, skill, ability. As the basis for the Wound, it suggests a lack of knowledge or the misuse of that knowledge or authority. In this case, I interpret this as my character's improper use of his ability, of his authority, his knowledge. The character himself has done the wrong and caused great harm, and this has inflicted his wound.

The second rune, Eihwaz, stands for the Yew tree and represents death and rebirth. This could be a literal or figurative death, but it indicates the dark night of the soul. In the place of the Identity, this works very well for my character in that the identity he has established for himself is that of the reformer, the judge. He holds the power to inflict death, purification, or transformation on those around him.

So, for the basis of this character we have a misuse of authority (his wound), which he tries to disguise by acting in the role of the judge and meting out punishment to those who may have misused their authority as well. This gives him a misplaced sense of transformation, of correcting his past mistakes. However it's not actually righting his wrongs, but simply creating a projection of his own self-judgment onto others.

Finally, we have Laguz. Laguz stands for emotion, life force energy. This rune represents the Essence of the character. If he is to become what he's meant to be, he must set aside the Identity of the lawgiver and embrace his emotions. He has to get in touch with his inner turmoil, his inner conflict. He must embrace these, which will pave the way for the next step in his evolution and allow for the healing of his wound.

The Web of Wyrd

THE NORSE IDEA OF DESTINY centered on the divine figures of the three Norns gathered about the Well of Urdh (Old English, Wyrd). Similar to the Greek Fates, the Norns collectively spun, wove, and cut the threads that formed the Web of Wyrd. The first of the Norns is Urdh, associated with the past, with foundations or primal energy. Verdandi stands for the present. Finally, Skuld represents outcome or debt.

Contrary to the fatalistic view that some have of the Norse mindset, the Norns represent a very practical notion of how the universe works. Urdh is etymologically associated with origins or orlog, which has a close connection with the Vedic dharma, meaning destiny or life-purpose. Verdandi represents not simply the present, but that which is becoming, the sequence of choices and circumstances that have led to the present unfolding of events. Skuld is closely linked to the word should. Rather than a carved-in-stone declaration of the future, she represents an extrapolation, a projection into the future of the current course of events and pattern of choices.

This runecasting is based on Odin's visit to the Well of Urdh, preceding his discovery of the Runes and the furtherance of his mission to humanity. The spread is best suited to scene- or sequence-level development, providing a snapshot of the character at a specific moment in the story. It may be used multiple times throughout your story development as a tool for enriching the story or getting unstuck.

Focus on the character or scene in question. Shuffle and cast the cards or tiles, and lay them out in the following arrangement:

(1) ODIN - THE SELF

This rune represents the character in the specific situation. It describes her mindset, her emotional condition, even the physical circumstances in which she finds herself.

(2) URDH - ORIGINS

This rune represents the series of circumstances that have brought the character to where she is. Whether real or perceived, this is how she believes she got to be where she is. It informs the past and/or her view of it.

(3) VERDANDI - BECOMING

Philosophers and self-help gurus broadly proclaim that there is only the present moment, the ever-becoming Now. The ancient Norse held a similar view. This rune stands for the experience, the present realization of the character within her situation. This is the Now, the Becoming of all the forces and events of the past into the present moment.

(4) SKULD - PROBABLE FUTURE

As with Karma (an Indo-European cousin to the Norse mindset), Skuld represents the likely or deserved outcome of the preceding, defining circumstances. This rune represents the trajectory of the previous two runes.

OPTIONAL EXPANSION

If the initial runecasting is vague or otherwise unsatisfactory, feel free to play around. For a specific casting, I recommend leaving the Odin and Urdh cards (1 & 2) as initially cast. Since Verdandi (3) represents the unfolding present and the Skuld rune (4) only indicates the likely outcome, this offers some flexibility.

To explore alternate plot points, flip over a new card and place it atop the (3) position. Then flip another card and place it over the (4) card. This represents a new choice or action on the part of your character and the likely, revised outcome.

Repeat this variation as needed. This offers a means to create suspense and surprise for your readers.

Sample Runecasting

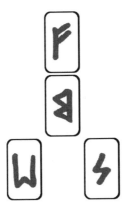

In this example, the Odin card—which represents the character within the scene—is Fehu. With the general interpretation of wealth, this suggests the character is well off, he has ample resources and has a great deal of potential or opportunity.

In the Urdh position is Ehwaz reversed. Ehwaz represents intuition or trust. Reversed, this suggests that the character has been acting contrary to his intuition or his gut feelings. He's been doing things that may be expedient or useful, but don't necessarily agree with his inner voice.

Next is Verdandi, the central position, which stands for what's happening now. Here, we have Berkano, also reversed. Berkano stands for life energy or nourishment. Reversed, it suggests illness or sickness. As it applies to my sample story, the character has become ill as an outgrowth of denying his intuition. He's acted contrary to what he knew on an inner level, and is now sick, possibly dying because of that.

Finally, we have Sowilo in the Skuld position. This is interesting because we have a fairly negative string of circumstances leading into this, but Sowilo—which means the Sun or soul, and generally indicates success—is a very benefic rune. So here we have the idea that through this string of experiences, somehow the soul is awakened and success is going to come. This layout, even though it seems contradictory, is perfect for the scene I have in mind.

If your runecasting doesn't seem to make sense, if it feels contradictory or goes too far, you may cast the optional expansion. Even though I'm quite happy with this runecasting, I've cast an alternate choice and outcome, as follows:

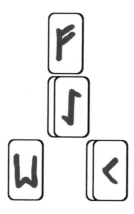

Here, the new Verdandi—an alternate choice—is represented by Eihwaz, which can't be reversed. Eihwaz means the yew tree and stands for radical, involuntary transformation. In the new Skuld position—the likely outcome of this alternate choice—we have Kenaz, which means torch and stands for knowledge, ability, and authority.

With this alternate scenario, we still have the character's abnegation of his intuition. Now this is followed by a radical transformation. This could be the character recognizing he needs to listen to his inner voice. As a result of this transformation—and in the case of this story, it may be a literal death and rebirth—he awakens to a new authority, a new knowledge and ability that can propel him into his new future.

The Five Elements

W HILE CLASSICAL MEDITERRANEAN cultures recognized four primal elements, the original Indo-European cosmogony included the fifth element, or quintessence. For the ancient Norse wise-ones (literally, wizards), these elements were Æther, Air, Fire, Water, and Earth. These correspond to the elements in Chinese and East Indian (Vedic) modalities, with the transposition of Wood for Æther, and Metal for Air.

In terms of density or consistency, Æther is the rarest of the elements. It represents the first expression of raw cosmic energy as it comes into manifestation. This is the element of expansion, of becoming.

Air is the first of the tangible elements, directly perceptible by touch, hearing, and smell. Only its effects can be observed by the other senses. This is the element of contraction, as the ethereal condenses into physicality.

Fire adds the sense of sight to direct perception. It is the rising element, even as flames rise from the hearth.

Water brings taste to the equation, as saliva awakens taste buds upon the tongue. This is the descending element, running downhill from source to sea, where it always finds its level.

Finally, Earth stands for the completion of the preceding elements.

The densest of all, it represents the center, the fixation of what has gone before.

The Five Elements runecasting is intended for a broader view than the Web of Wyrd, and is best suited to the Sequence or Act, possibly the entire story from a thematic viewpoint. The order of the runes is based on directional associations rather than density.

(Note that the directions of this casting are based on the ancient Indo-European worldview of North as down and South as up. If you're more comfortable with the modern convention, you may place the second card above the center, and proceed clockwise.)

Focus on the sequence or story in question. Shuffle and cast the cards or tiles, and lay them out in the following arrangement:

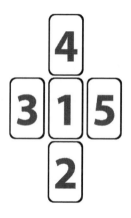

(1) EARTH - CHARACTER

As in the Web of Wyrd runecasting, the first card represents the character in the particular situation, the experiential world. Though relatively dense and fixed, it can be impacted by the workings of the other elements. As the culmination of all the other elements, Earth finds its place in the center.

(2) WATER - RESTRAINING FORCES

This rune stands for those elements (characters, circumstances, etc.) that seek to maintain the status quo. This is water seeking its own level, those forces that seek equanimity, stasis. As water combines with earth to form clay, this rune represents those forces that seek to keep the character and/or situation as-is. Directionally, Water is associated with the North.

(3) ÆTHER - EXPANSIVE POWER

The Æther rune represents the forces that seek to raise the character to her highest potential. Think Robin Williams's character Sean Maguire in *Good Will Hunting*. Your character may not always appreciate the influence or input of this rune, but the ultimate aim is for her highest good. Directionally, Æther is associated with the East.

(4) FIRE - ACTIVATING FORCES

Fire is a motive force that changes one condition into another. Wood transforms into ash, metal or ice becomes liquid, liquid turns to vapor. In the process, heat and light are released to provide comfort and guidance, or possibly destruction. This rune kicks the character out of complacency and into action. It could show up in the invigorating strength of a good meal, or in the jarring suddenness of a house fire. Regardless, the character must move, and things will never be the same again. Directionally, Fire is associated with the South.

(5) AIR - CONTRACTING POWER

Like a cool breeze on a summer evening, the force behind this rune seeks the ultimate comfort and sensual pleasure of the character. This energy is that of the mother who seeks comfort and ease for her child, even if that means he can't quite achieve his full potential—regardless, he'll be safe from harm. Not a bad place to be, but it lacks the ultimate fulfillment of Æther. Directionally, Air is associated with the West.

Sample Runecasting

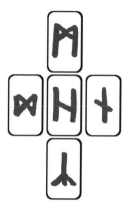

The center of this runecasting represents the Earth element, the present situation of the scene, or the character within the scene. Here, we have Hagalaz, which literally means hail and stands for purification. As mentioned in the discussion of Hagalaz, this purification may be as gentle as snowfall or as devastating as a hailstorm, depending on how the character receives it. For my story and my character, this is not going to be pleasant.

In the Water position is Elhaz reversed. Elhaz literally means elk and is interpreted as protection or alignment. Reversed, this suggests the character is resisting the purification that's in store for him, and he's stuck in the role of the dark shaman, the sorcerer. He's been contradicting or actively opposing the forces of nature and, rather than offering protection, is causing harm. If he is to move forward, to develop as a character and attain his goal, he must break the cycle and receive his purification.

We move now to the Æther element. Here, we have Dagaz, which literally means day and stands for balance and order. This suggests that if order can be established, this will result in the highest good for the character and for the situation. Our character must realign himself with the natural cycle, the natural harmony, and the situation will result in the greatest good.

In the element of Fire is Mannaz upright. Mannaz means a human being, and its root is shared with the words mind and Moon. It can be interpreted as a healthy mental condition, but it also suggests a recognition of shared humanity, of seeing oneself reflected in another. There's a very cooperative aspect to this, a notion of unity. In the Fire element, as the activating principle, the recognition of this unity and cooperation will move the story into its next sequence. Interestingly—and this tends to be how it works out—we had the opposite sense of this in the Water element. Elhaz reversed, which indicates vulnerability or the misuse of power, is keeping the situation stagnant, is resisting the needed purification. Here in the Fire position, it is the recognition of shared humanity, of shared essence that will allow the purification to take place and the scene to move forward.

Now we have the element of Air. In this position we have Nauthiz, which means need or necessity, and suggests a bow-drill that can be used to make fire. In the position of contracting forces, of those seeking the greatest comfort for the character, in my particular scene it suggests a good meal by the fire and a warm bed, as opposed to going out into the cold and the darkness that might lead to a greater transformation. The warmth of this rune, of the campfire, will bring comfort and sustenance to my character but may limit his purification.

The Nine Worlds

NORSE COSMOLOGY CENTERS on the great World Tree, Yggdrasil, which contains among its roots and branches the nine realms of manifest reality. From the heights of Asgard—fortress of the Celestial Deities—to the depths of Hella's Home, the loftiest and lowest aspirations of man or giant or god bear fruit upon the tree.

This casting is best used in the formative stages of a project. Alternately, if you are well into a story and find yourself absolutely stuck—assuming the fear of abandonment is greater than the fear of a major rewrite—it can give a fresh outlook on the story's potential.

Best used with a premise in mind—perhaps seasoned with a few milestone scenes, but before specifics of character, conflict, or outcomes are established—this pattern combines the Norse cosmology with the Hero's Journey, as outlined by Joseph Campbell and further distilled by Christopher Vogler.

The central rune represents a static condition, the situation from which the story begins. The surrounding runes represent major story elements. They may be taken sequentially (for example, 2 & 3 as Act I, 4 - 7 as Act II, 8 & 9 as Act III), or interwoven as you see fit.

This runecasting is based on the ancient reckoning of North as down, South as up. If you prefer the modern convention, you may place the second card above the center, then proceed in a clockwise fashion.

Focus on the story in question. Shuffle and cast the cards or tiles, and lay them out in the following arrangement:

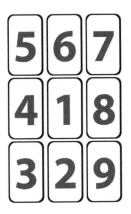

(1) MIDGARD - ORDINARY WORLD

In Norse cosmology, Midgard is simply our Earth, the realm of ordinary human existence. As such, the central card establishes the protagonist in her ordinary, static circumstances at the beginning of the story. This is her day-to-day experience of the real world with all its burdens of conflict, ease, and boredom.

(2) NIFLHEIM - OPPORTUNITY

According to the myths, Niflheim (Mist Home) was one of the first realms to come into existence, along with Muspelheim (Fire Home). As sparks from Muspelheim leapt across the void of Ginungagap (the Yawning Chasm), ice melted, evaporated, condensed, and froze again. After countless cycles of this dance between fire and ice, eventually a briny solution formed out of which arose the first life in our universe.

With this sense of coming out of nothingness, and drawing from Michael Hauge's *Story Mastery*, the rune in this position represents Something New, a break from ordinary reality. This is not the beginning of the new story, but an awakening of the protagonist from her stasis in Midgard, a glimpse of something new among the mists of her formative existence.

(3) ASGARD - GLIMPSE OF POTENTIAL

One of the better known realms of Norse myth, Asgard is the fortress of the Aesir, the Celestial Deities who embody such ethereal qualities as truth, honor, loyalty, wisdom. This realm is typically associated with the Northeast. Whereas Niflheim represents infinite, unmanifest potential, Asgard stands for the perfection that has just manifested into physical being.

With respect to your story, out of the awakening of the Opportunity comes a brand new world. In *The Wizard of Oz*, Dorothy chases after Miss Gulch, who has abducted Toto, only to be sucked up into the tornado and drawn into Oz, where nothing is as it was before. This represents the Inciting Incident of your story and/or Crossing the Threshold.

(4) JOTUNHEIM - FORCES OF ANTAGONISM

In the Norse legends, the East represented Jotunheim, or Giant Home. This is where mighty Thor frequently went for battle and sport. Contrary to the giants of later fables, the denizens of Jotunheim were not all mindless brutes. Several of the Aesir and Vanir were smitten by beautiful giantesses, or coveted their wisdom. In one of the more popular myths, we find Thor engaged in a contest of strength and appetite against a number of the giants. Though he fails to win, we discover this was because he was competing not against mere mortal beings, but against the very forces of nature such as time, the tides, old age, and even gravity.

The rune in this position, then, represents those forces that oppose our hero as she sets out on her journey. Not necessarily a sequence in and of itself, it stands for those events and characters that oppose the protagonist's progress and which—by virtue of the tension they inspire—propel the story forward.

(5) SVARTALFHEIM - MENTORS, ALLIES & TOOLS

Located in the Southeast, Svartalfheim is the traditional home of the Dwarfs or Dark Elves, craftsmen of the gods. Thor's hammer (Mjolnir) and Odin's spear (Gungnir) both have their origins in this realm. Coincidentally (or not), both were crafted at the instigation (and to the consternation) of Loki, the shapeshifter/trickster who keeps the old myths interesting and relevant.

Similarly, the rune in this position represents those story elements that aid the hero in her quest. This may represents an individual (such as a Mentor or Fairy Godmother figure), a tool or weapon, or a general characteristic of her helpers. Upright, this rune may signify a power or alliance that will assist the protagonist through the second act. If reversed, it may suggest a weakness in her character that needs to be corrected before she can become all the awesomeness she is.

(6) MUSPELHEIM - ACTIVATING FORCE

As alluded to above, the Southern realm of Muspelheim (Fire Home) provided the activating force that sparked physical creation out of the infinite potential of Niflheim. In a similar manner, the rune in this position typically leads us to the midpoint of the story, the fabled Point of No Return. Here the forces of antagonism, change, and support all culminate in a sequence or moment of transformation. Circumstances force the hero from reactive to proactive behavior. There is no going back, and things will never be as they were before.

(7) HELHEIM - ULTIMATE TRANSFORMATION

Though often equated with the christianized Hell, the Norse Hel (or Hella's Home) was the place of reflection and contemplation between lives, similar to the Greek Tartarus or Hebrew Sheol. Associated with the Southwest, this is the realm of separation from who we once were, a place of abandoning both hope and fear.

This position represents the Dark Night of the Soul, the hero's experience of ultimate transformation. Allies have fallen away, the antagonist appears to be winning, and the protagonist is faced with stark reality. The choice is between the oblivion of the grave and a new way of viewing and navigating the world.

(8) VANAHEIM - OBTAINING THE BOON

Norse mythology describes a primordial war between the Aesir of Asgard and the Vanir, or terrestrial deities, who reside in the Western realm of Vanaheim. Whereas the Aesir are associated more with abstract ideas and ideals, the Vanir are deities of all aspects of earthly existence. These are the gods of agriculture, fertility, weather, travel, trade, etc.

This eighth rune, then, stands for the story's climax, the aim of the Hero's Journey. This is what it all means. All she's experienced, all the trials and tribulations, the victories and defeats coalesce into this moment, scene, or sequence. This is the object of the quest, the boon or balm that will bring health and hope to the tribe.

(9) LJOSSALFHEIM - THE RETURN

Positioned in the Northwest, Ljossalfheim (Light-Elf Home) represents the culmination of the story. The Light Elves are variously associated with the Western ideal of Ascended Masters, and with the indigenous notion of the Ancestors who guide and advise those of us still on a physical journey.

This rune represents the denouement and the outcome of the hero's Return to the Ordinary World (Midgard) with the boon. Reversed, and depending on genre and theme, it may indicate the hero's reluctance, refusal, or failure to complete the Return.

Sample Runecasting

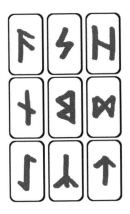

For my story example, we have in the center—in Midgard, the Ordinary World—Berkano reversed. Berkano is the birch tree and indicates nourishment and vitality. Reversed, it suggests that the ordinary world is one of sickness, of disease, of not being cared for. For this story, I see it as a blighted land. Crops are failing. There's drought, famine, misery. Not a happy scene, but this is the Ordinary World in which the story begins.

Next, in the North of Niflheim, is the Opportunity. This is the first recognition that things don't necessarily have to be this way. This is that first push off of center for the character. In this case, we have Elhaz reversed. For my story, I choose to interpret this rune as the protector, the shaman—in this case, my protagonist. Being inverted, this suggests the first realization that, because he has not been fulfilling his role, he has made his people vulnerable and perhaps he is the cause of this blight that is on the land. He's not yet taking action on this, but this realization begins to put the story into motion.

In the northeast is the realm of Asgard. This is a view of the potential. This is the Inciting Incident and the change that really sets the story into motion. Here, we have Eihwaz, the yew tree and the rune of dramatic, often involuntary, transformation. For my story, this transformation shows up as a deposition or removal from office for the main character. Because he's allowed the land to go into blight, because he has failed in his position as the protector of his world, he is cast out. He is transformed from what he was into something very different. Now, the story is in motion.

Next is the Eastern realm of Jotunheim, which represents the Forces of Antagonism. Here we have Nauthiz, which means need, necessity, or innovation. In this case, it appears that the story problem and my character's reaction—his intellectual problem-solving response—is actually going to hinder him. Trying to innovate a solution will get in the way and create more harm than good as he moves through the story.

We next come to the Southeast and the realm of Svartalfheim. This is the position of Allies and Helpers, and we have Ansuz, which stands for the Aesir and suggests divine communication or inspiration. Contrary to the previous rune of innovation or intellectual problem-solving—which will derail my protagonist—his greatest help in moving through this story is going to be inspiration. His help will come more through his intuition or messages from the divine.

Next comes the South and Muspelheim. This is the activating element, the inner spark that establishes the Point of No Return and will propel the protagonist to the end of the story. In this case, we have Sowilo. The means the Sun and also represents the soul. This rune can also be interpreted as success. This suggests a scene where my protagonist, rather than acting out of habits or knee-jerk reactions, responds in a way that comes from his soul, that comes from his highest being. In acting from his soul, in being guided by his inner light, he will find the means to succeed.

We are now in the Southwest and the realm of Helheim. In terms of story structure, this is the deep, dark moment. This is when the character comes face-to-face with reality. Here, we have Hagalaz, which literally means hail and implies purification. As mentioned previously, this purification may be welcome or resisted, gentle or torturous. As we're in the All-Is-Lost moment—and coming out of the soul activation of the Point of No Return—this suggests my character recognizes his need to be purified, his need to let go of what has been. This is my protagonist giving in to that purification. It's not likely to be pleasant, but it will be a natural outgrowth of his soul revelation from the preceding rune. This will awaken my hero to his new way of being.

It's interesting to note that, diagonally opposite in the Inciting Incident, we had the rune of involuntary transformation, which kicked the story into motion. Here we have the purification rune, its counterpart, in the position that's going to bring the story to its conclusion. It's a beautiful, lovely balance and perfectly fits the mythic scope of this particular story.

Now we move into the West and Vanaheim, the home of the terrestrial deities. This position represents the Boon, and here we have Dagaz, which can actually be interpreted as a reward or balance. Dagaz is at home in the West, and this reinforces the strength of this interpretation. The reward is in finding this balance, in bringing the land, the kingdom back into harmony.

Finally, we have the Northwestern realm of Ljossalfheim. This is the home of the Light Elves, of the elders, the ancestors, or the Ascended Masters. This represents the Return, and here we have the rune Tiwaz. Tiwaz stands for the god Tyr and represents honor, forthrightness, integrity. So, we have this character who should have been in this role initially, the role of the protective shaman. He's experienced all these transformations and purifications, has retrieved the Boon that will restore balance to the land, and now stands renewed in the position of the honorable defender of his realm.

Curious to see how the story shapes up? How the Runes inform the narrative? Take a peek at *Odin's Tale* at the end of the book.

Going Beyond

On Creativity and Writer's Block

U NDERSTANDING HOW TO MOST effectively use the *Runes for Writers* system requires at least a cursory knowledge of the nature of creativity. Now, a storyteller doesn't have to know all the intricacies of consciousness and the human mind any more than someone has to be an auto mechanic to drive a car. Should the car break down, however, a mechanic will have a decided advantage in getting unstuck and back on the road than the run-of-the-mill driver. Similarly, the storyteller who understands how the creative process works will be far more skilled in keeping her creative engine in top form and getting back on track should things go awry.

The first thing to understand is the nature of human consciousness. A human being operates on at least nine different levels of consciousness. Some of these we share in common with animals and so-called lower lifeforms. Other levels of consciousness are distinctly human, while others we share with beings on an even higher evolutionary scale.

Fair warning, this discussion may seem a bit *woo-woo*, but the principles we'll be exploring have been understood by truly integrated human beings for thousands of generations. Jung and Freud and later depth psychologists caught glimpses of these truths and brought them closer to the mainstream. Today, neuroscientists and quantum physicists are beginning to formulate theories to span the gulf between the inner and outer worlds that the wise ones have known for millennia. If I seem to be leading you into the deep esoteric woods, just stick with me and trust we'll all come out safe on the other side.

With regard to Story, we're mainly concerned with the Ordinary Consciousness, the Subconscious, and the Unconscious Mind. The Superconscious and Higher Consciousness also come into play, but these primarily interact with the Unconscious. For the scope of this practice, we'll just stick with the first three.

The Ordinary Consciousness is that level of awareness we normally associate with everyday waking consciousness. This is the active mind that thinks and feels and interacts with the world around you.

The Unconscious Mind is deeply hidden within the psyche, but is the single most powerful level of consciousness for physical beings. When we hear the adage that we only use 5-10% of our brains (really, our Minds), the Unconscious Mind takes up the vast majority of the other 90-95%. Neuroscientists posit that the brain receives upward of eleven million pieces of information every second. To put this in perspective, if each piece of information were worth one cent, the neural input to the United States populous would pay off the national debt in just over half a second. A penny for your thoughts?

Now, we're obviously not aware of all this information. If even one percent of that data made it into the Ordinary Consciousness, we'd all be catatonic from sensory overload. But every one of these data points is received, archived, spindled, and mutilated by the Unconscious Mind. This is the ultimate data storage facility, the clearinghouse of human experience.

The Subconscious Mind acts as the research librarian, the go-between from the Unconscious Mind to the Ordinary Consciousness. The information retrieved rests in the Ordinary Consciousness for a time (the short-term memory bin), before being returned to its place in the stacks. Repetition of certain thought patterns (physically represented by synaptic pathways in the brain) boosts the efficiency of recall, such as for birthdays, telephone numbers, driving directions, etc.

Those inputs that are beneficial for physical survival—for example, the screech of brakes and blare of the horn from a truck barreling down on you—are given priority status. These may be relayed to the Ordinary Consciousness—or, more likely, straight to the brain stem—for immediate processing and action. The importance granted and the speed of transmission goes rapidly downhill from there. The location of your car keys and that great story idea you had last night are relatively low on the file clerk's priority list. Which leads us back to the point of this book and the *Runes for Writers* system.

If you're anything like me, you've misplaced your keys on more than one occasion. You're in a rush for work or a dinner appointment, and *Poof!*—Gremlins have made off with your keys. You systematically search the house, you retrace your steps since last arriving at home, all to no avail. You wrack your Ordinary Consciousness—intellect, short-term memory, logical processing—in an effort to locate those pesky keys, but nothing seems to work.

The problem in this case is that we're using the wrong tool—the wrong level of consciousness—for the job. It wasn't the Ordinary Consciousness that left the keys wherever they might be. It wasn't the intellect, reason, or even emotional choice that hid them. Yet we generally resort to those levels of consciousness to find a solution to the situation created by another.

Instead, it's only after you've canceled your plans, sat down on the sofa, and punched up Netflix that the solution appears. You're bingeing *The Last Kingdom*, and your Subconscious whispers to your Ordinary Consciousness, *Gee, some ice cream would be great right about now.* You may debate this among your various levels of consciousness but—again, if you're anything like me—higher judgment prevails and you head to the freezer. And there you discover your keys, right next to the ice tray where you left them.

The point here is that it wasn't the Ordinary Consciousness that chose to deposit the keys along with the Alden's. And it isn't the Ordinary Consciousness that can unravel the bizarre yet deliciously satisfying sequence of events that led to their recovery.

The same is true with writer's block. It's a common fallacy among creatives that our brilliance is a product of superior intellect, that our Genius (in its Classical meaning) arises from the Ordinary

Consciousness. If this were the case, the Ordinary Consciousness would be the perfect tool for getting unstuck when our stories go off the rails and we have no idea what to write next.

Fact of the matter, Story arises from the Unconscious Mind. It actually has its origins outside of any individual human experience, but its appearance within the milieu of the individual storyteller comes through the Unconscious Mind. From there, as time and diet and other matters of physical survival allow, the Subconscious is able to ferry bits and pieces of a particular story into the conscious awareness of said storyteller.

When those threads of the story taper off, or when the Ordinary Consciousness has taken over for Flow and written itself into a corner, we experience the condition commonly referred to as Writer's Block—capital letters, italics, boldface, and any other sort of nefarious emphasis with which you care to embellish it.

Thus blocked, we typically then turn to the Intellect, that agent of the Ordinary Consciousness, to craft a solution. We storyboard, conduct character interviews, observe and analyze hapless bystanders at the mall or the dog park. All to no avail, because we're enlisting the wrong center of consciousness to resolve the problem. If we want to reconnect to the Story, we need to return to its Source in the Unconscious Mind.

Which leads us to...

How All This Stuff Works

THE SOURCE OF STORY—of any story—resides outside of the human brain, beyond the Ordinary Consciousness or any event related to the particular storyteller. Now, an idea may seem to spring from a personal experience, but its evolution into a story that might have any relevance to another individual passes through a realm far removed from our everyday experience. Such stories exist independently of the storyteller.

Plato called this source the Realm of Ideas. This was a place where the idea, for example, of an oak tree had its origins. The oak trees that we see and experience are simply drawing material from the physical world and accreting that, bringing it together and growing within some matrix that comes from this Realm of Ideas. But the ideal, the primeval Oak Tree—the template for all oak trees to come—resides in this non-physical realm.

Jung spoke about this to some degree in his theory of the Collective Unconscious. Here he offered the idea that there are experiences, realities, and understandings that reside outside of the individual, and that we can access these through the Subconscious. Even Joseph Campbell touched on this aspect of creativity when he spoke of the Monomyth, the idea that the structure of story among cultures separated by vast quantities of time and space, are eerily similar.

When you create, when you have that flash of inspiration, you're reaching into this non-physical realm. Your Unconscious Mind absorbs these data—along with the eleven million bits per second you receive from your physical environment—and faithfully stores them away. Your Subconscious is then able to retrieve these from that realm and bring the story to the attention of your Conscious Mind.

Of course, you're not simply a medium. You're not a mere channel, but a partner in the creation of the story. Story itself is beyond language. It is beyond movement, beyond symbol. It's beyond anything of the physical world. It is the abstract notion of any particular story. In order for that story to be accessible, to be communicable to other people, requires the intervention of the artist, the storyteller. Story needs you.

You receive the story—however fine or bold the brush strokes—then translate it into language, into motion, into some vehicle through which the story can be conveyed to other human beings. It's a vital partnership. Story arises when its time is ripe, and it selects the storyteller who can best convey its essence into thought and language.

All well and good. But what does this have to do with writer's block, and how can this system help you and your story?

Quite simply, writer's block is never the fault of Story. Your muse, your daemon, your inspiration is sitting patiently by, waiting to upload the next installment of Genius. The problem is that the Intellect, the Ordinary Consciousness, has adopted the story as its own and chosen to run with it. Usually, straight into a corner. And the more you cogitate, the more you outline and analyze and brainstorm, the harder your Ordinary Consciousness bounces off the brick wall.

Rather than trying to counter this innate reaction, *Runes for Writers* works with the various levels of consciousness and their root functions, not against them. Visual cues, writing prompts, and similar creativity jump-starters do engage the creativity center, but their overt imagery and meanings leave little for the Intellect to chew on, so it simply tries to create linear, logical links between the surface prompts and the story problem.

By contrast, the abstract nature of the Runes distracts the Intellect as it tries to identify the shape, name, sound value, and other properties associated with the particular rune. With the left brain thus distracted, the right brain can sneak past the intellectual musings and connect directly with the underlying, multi-dimensional symbolism of the Runes that reside in the realms of the Unconscious Mind. And it is here, within the Unconscious Mind, that the solution to any particular story problem (or life problem, for that matter) resides.

All genuine divinatory systems—and the Runes, Tarot, dowsing, pendulums, and so forth all began as divinatory systems—find their value by the manner in which they connect the user to her Unconscious Mind. As described above, the personal Unconscious Mind gathers and sorts every bit of information we're exposed to—thousands or millions of times what actually gets passed along to the Ordinary Consciousness. This is hard science.

What is less well developed (though quantum physics is drawing nearer to a proof—well, as much a proof as the Uncertainty Principle will permit) is the premise that each individual Unconscious Mind floats in the stream of the Collective Unconscious, as described by Jung. Here, not only is it possible to access every bit of information we've personally been exposed to, but to access all the information that is. Period.

That's a lot. And while it takes many lifetimes to approach the level where such information can be accessed at will, the ability to retrieve the solution to a personally relevant problem—particularly a problem relevant to a story you've been called to write—can be acquired in very short order.

The Subconscious, then, is the key to accessing Story. Whether the inspiration arises from the Collective Unconscious or is sparked by the Muses and Guides who live in the Superconscious realms, your story resides within your personal Unconscious Mind. The Subconscious shuttles back and forth with the appropriate bits of story at just the right time.

If you run into a block, it's generally due to a conflict between your Intellect and Unconscious. This may manifest as pure Resistance (a slightly different animal than what we're addressing here) or it may be that the Intellect is looking for one piece of information while the Subconscious knows the story needs something else. If we can get the Intellect out of the way and build a mutual trust with the Subconscious, that part of the mind will become our greatest ally in bringing Story into complete and glorious manifestation.

The power of the Runes is in freeing the Subconscious to dive deep and come back with inspiration from the Unconscious. The Unconscious Mind itself already knows every aspect of your story, both to deliver an engaging tale and to relay the more important thematic, transformative message. If you get stuck, it's simply a matter of distracting the Intellect and freeing the Subconscious and Unconscious Minds to work together to bring you the answers you seek.

A Peek Behind the Curtain

NOUGH WITH THE NERD STUFF. How do the Runes and other divinatory systems actually work? Is there truly magic afoot? Spooky action at a distance? What?

If you recall from the previous section, the Unconscious Mind has access to every piece of information you have personally experienced and—if Jung was right—every piece of information that has ever been (or could be) experienced. Whenever you're stuck in a story—you don't know what the next scene should be, you've written yourself into a corner, or you simply don't know what the story is—your Unconscious Mind has the solution. The trick is to get that information into your Ordinary Consciousness, the part of you that actually brings the words onto the page.

Enter the Subconscious, your best friend and partner in this thing called Storytelling.

As in our example of the car keys, the Subconscious knows exactly where the solution to your story problem lies. It knows the exact story element, conflict, or turn of phrase you need to elevate the story and lead seamlessly into the next sequence. The challenge is how to retrieve the information and sneak it past the watchdog Intellect.

We've likened the Subconscious to a file clerk or research librarian, but there's one aspect we haven't touched on yet. In addition to retrieving information from the inner world of your Unconscious Mind, the Subconscious can also project experiences and conditions into the outer world. You've probably experienced this in more or less welcome circumstances.

You've signed up for a writer's conference where the agent who represents your literary idol is scheduled to appear. You think this could be *It*—but do you really? Inside, you're a mess. Your manuscript isn't nearly good enough. You can hardly write your own name, let alone the next Great American Novel. You think your parents may have been right and you should stick to auto repair. The faithful Subconscious is there to provide the answer you think you want, your very own Magic Genie. Your alarm doesn't go off, and you have to scramble to get to the airport on time. That's okay, because your flight is delayed—and delayed and delayed and then canceled. You catch an alternate flight but arrive at the conference hotel around O-dark-thirty. Your luggage never made the transfer, so you have a hotel bathrobe and some moist-wipes to see you through the first day of conference. Still not to worry, because your dream agent had to cancel her appearance due to a rare case of the shingles.

Alternately, you've signed up for the same conference and a pitch with the same agent. You're confident in your story and yourself. You awaken three minutes before your alarm. Zero traffic, and you breeze through airport security with plenty of time to stop at Cinnabon before boarding your plane, where you have the whole row to yourself. The hotel made a mistake with your reservation and upgrades you to a premium suite. You happen to run into Dream Agent while relaxing in the hotel bar and she asks for the full manuscript then and there.

In both of these scenarios (or anywhere along the continuum), the Subconscious is busy at work carrying out your instructions, for the good or ill of your actual intent. Some of these impacts are within your control: You set the alarm correctly or you don't; you pick the right security line or not; you choose to socialize or hole up in your room. Some seem to have nothing to do with you: Traffic, flight delays, other people being in the right place or frame of mind or state of health. But even these are the result of the Subconscious as it relays information to your personal Unconscious Mind, which then—through the network of the Collective Unconscious—relays information to the Unconscious Minds of others directly or indirectly related to your particular mission and underlying desire on any given day.

In this respect, the Subconscious takes a much more outwardly active role. Not simply a clerk, it is the concierge, the curator, your own personal butler. It is the Alfred to your Batman.

And it's in this role that the very magic of the Runes and other divinatory systems comes into effect.

We've seen how the Unconscious Mind takes in every bit of information around you, the vast majority of which never makes it to your Ordinary Consciousness. This includes the cards, tiles, or dice you use for your runecasting. The indentations in the dice, subtle imperfections or irregularities in the cards and tiles. Even as you shuffle or shake the runes to randomize them, the Unconscious Mind tracks the location of each one, and the Subconscious Mind quietly and expertly stacks the deck.

You can make this process as mystical or as pedestrian as you like. The fact is simply that your Unconscious Mind has the key to any story challenge you might possibly face. By acknowledging this and by providing a method of communication in agreed-upon language and symbols, and by temporarily sidelining your Intellect, you open the channels of communication so that those solutions can come to the realization of your Ordinary Consciousness.

Becoming a Shaman of Story

N OW THAT WE UNDERSTAND how the mind works to put a story together, how do we use this to empower our storytelling?

Empower and engage all levels of your consciousness.

An active intellectual and emotional life—the hallmarks of the Ordinary Consciousness—is crucial to navigating the day-to-day world of work, relationships, and surviving in physical form. It's also important to open yourself to the inspirations of the Superconscious Mind through art, uplifting reading, and other activities that allow for higher forms of thought and awareness. Equally important is exercising the Subconscious and strengthening your connection to the Unconscious Mind through meditation, free writing, practice with the Runes, and so on.

REDUCE YOUR STRESS

Stress triggers the Ordinary Consciousness, which works in real time to craft solutions to keep us alive, to the exclusion of all other aspects of the mind. It trains the Subconscious to relay only those pieces of information necessary for survival, to the exclusion of trivialities such as creativity, higher ideals, etc. We live in a world shaped to keep us in a constant state of stress and so lock us into the Intellect. Removing or reducing stress (turning off the news is a good start) allows the Intellect to take a breather and gives you greater freedom to engage with the deeper and more subtle realms of your consciousness.

STAY HEALTHY

This is a corollary to the previous item. The healthier you are, the less stress is on the physical mechanism of your body, and the more the Intellect can relax. Get plenty of rest, fresh air, and natural light. Exercise and eat wholesome foods. Play with your pet and spend time with loved ones. All these things will improve your general health and just make you happier. Who doesn't need that?

DEVELOP A MINDFULNESS PRACTICE

As with the shamanic practices of old, storytelling is a sacred art. Take time out from busy-ness every day to sit, reflect, pray, meditate, or simply listen to your heartbeat and your breath. Any practice that connects you to your inner self and that helps you center on your place in the world will be time well spent.

Studies suggest that fifteen to twenty minutes of meditation has the restorative effect of a few hours of sleep or even an entire day off work. In addition to lowering stress and cortisol, meditation gives you the opportunity to listen for the whisperings of the Unconscious Mind and the inspirations of the Superconscious.

BUILD YOUR SHAMANIC TOOLKIT

While strengthening the connections among the various aspects of your mind will help proof you against writer's block, your stories will still not simply write themselves. There will still come times when you hit an impasse, when your characters are being stubborn, or when you're just not sure what should happen next.

While *Runes for Writers* and other divinatory tools can give great results the first time out of the box, your facility with them will grow with regular use. Build your rapport with the Runes through daily or weekly practice. You might even create a ritual around their use such as lighting a candle, burning incense, or simply casting them on a special cloth. Ritual, however simple or complex, signals the Subconscious and Unconscious Minds that it is their time and that they may freely communicate with your Ordinary Consciousness. With regular practice, they'll quickly learn that you're serious about connecting with them, and those lines of creative communication will gain strength.

GIVE YOUR GIFT TO THE WORLD

Story has the power to transform lives and shape our world. The world needs your story and your unique way of presenting it. The more you give of that gift, the more the Muse will see you as a vital partner in breathing life into Story, and the more ideas and inspiration she'll send your way.

Stories don't come along by accident. When the Collective Unconscious needs a concept to be brought into greater awareness, that story is given to the artist or artists who can best do so. There may be any number of stories across multiple types of media that relay the same notion. And Story has chosen you to share the laughter, the inspiration, the enjoyment, and the message that only you can give.

Go forth and be glorious.

Odin's Tale

Runes for Writers **in Practice**

THE FOLLOWING SHORT STORY is based on the sample runecastings presented in Part Three, *The Journey Back*. The source of the tale springs from the *Havamal*, found in *The Codex Regius*. This collection of Old Norse poetry was compiled in thirteenth-century Iceland.

The text in question consists of a mere eight stanzas, yet it portrays one of the most significant events in Norse mythology: the discovery of the Runes by the god Odin. With only this fragment of a story as its basis, the sample runecastings filled in the details of character, scene, and the overall shape of this short story.

The story, of course, is brief to fit the scope of this book. If I'd intended to publish it as a stand-alone story, I would certainly have taken more care with style and character development. As it stands, the tale is meant to serve as an example of how *Runes for Writers* can be used to help authors craft their stories from only the smallest fragments of an idea.

Beyond the core text, this tale includes certain philosophical symbolism to reflect a deeper sense of Norse shamanism. I've flagged the text to mark specific sections that directly pertain to the runecastings.

Excerpt from *The Havamal*

140. I know that I hung, on a wind-rocked tree, nine whole nights, with a spear wounded, and to Odin offered, myself to myself; on that tree, of which no one knows from what root it springs.

141. Bread no one gave me, nor a horn of drink, downward I peered, to runes applied myself, wailing learnt them, then fell down thence.

142. Potent songs nine from the famed son I learned of Bolthorn, Bestla's sire, and a draught obtained of the precious mead, drawn from Odhrærir.

143. Then I began to bear fruit, and to know many things, to grow and well thrive: word by word I sought out words, fact by fact I sought out facts.

144. Runes thou wilt find, and explained characters, very large characters, very potent characters, which the great speaker depicted, and the high powers formed, and the powers' prince graved.

Odin's Tale

Five Elements,
Earth | Nine Ele-
ments, Niflheim.
Shaman/protector
shirking his duties

I STAGGER DOWN THE ROAD, staff in hand, the words of my accusers pealing in my ears.

Wastrel.

Failure.

Outcast.

A cold wind hastens me on my way, and I pull my thin, grey cloak more tightly about my shoulders. The cloud-blotted sun slips behind the distant mountains, taking its meager light and warmth from me. Its setting mirrors my own decline, and I choke with laughter at the irony.

Web of Wyrd,
Odin. Beginning
from a position of
great wealth

Only this morning I was a king, master of many lands and lord over many people. Yes, those lands had been blighted of late. And, yes, those people had gone hungry that their meager harvests should keep my larder full. But was that my fault?

Nine Worlds, Mid-
gard. But the land
is wasted

According to my brothers—according even to my own wife—the answer is Yes.

A spatter of rain dampens my cheek. I look up to see great, roiling clouds clot the darkening sky. Lightning ripples within the gloom, and I wonder if my son is sending me a message.

Odin's Lots,
Wound. The
adopted Identity
of the Sage is no
longer working

Before I can think further on this, the sky's belly bursts open. Sheets of water pour from the heavens, quickly turning the road into a morass.

I seek shelter, but the barren trees offer no protection. A rocky scarp borders the road ahead, a broad overhang promising some little shelter. As quickly as the sucking

Five Elements,
Earth. Purification
begins

mud will allow, I slog toward it, my staff as much punting pole as walking stick.

The rocks are slick with rain. My first try at climbing up from the flooded track sees my muddy foot slip. I fall onto the stone, gashing my chin and gnashing my teeth. I mutter a curse, and deep from the heart of the rock I feel a rumble of laughter, as from Jord herself.

Half-blinded by the downpour, I peel myself from the rock. I plant my staff and, with greater care, resume my climb toward shelter.

The overhang protects but a shallow fold in the rock. I press myself into the farthest corner, my sodden cloak and robes clinging to me. The shelter spares me from the worst of the rain, though I am still spattered by rebounding drops and occasional gusts. Still, I breathe a sigh of relief.

My solace proves premature as a trickle of water leeches along the ceiling of the overhang. The trickle turns to a rivulet, invading my haven. The one is joined by a dozen more until the rainfall within the shelter is nearly as intolerable as that without.

I squeeze into the deepest corner, contracting and contorting my body to avoid the worst of the waterfalls. And then bad-gone-worse becomes worse still.

The flood outside reaches the level of my rocky redoubt. Water breaches the gate and storms over my palisades. What I had taken for solid earth beneath me begins to melt away as snowdrifts beneath the spring-time sun.

A chasm opens in the floor, grows and grows until its maw yawns as wide as Ginungagap. I press more tightly against the rock wall, but there is no escape. The soaked earth falls away beneath me, and I plunge, screaming, into the void.

ᚺ

Five Elements, Earth. And the purification continues...

ʃ

Nine Worlds, Asgard. The Void is the ultimate realm of transformation

L AUGHTER BUBBLES around me. Cackles ring out from all sides. A wheezing snigger sounds in one ear as moist breath dampens my cheek.

Nine Worlds, Svartalfheim. Though unknown to our protagonist, these figures with an ear to the divine will be his great allies and mentors

"It lives," says a rasping voice, scraped raw by time.

"A pity," chimes in another voice, softer and distinctly feminine. "Kill it."

"Don't be a fool," yet a third voice says, grandmotherly in her chastisement. "Nothing tastes so sweet as living flesh peeled from the bones."

The laughter resumes, and a sharp-nailed finger pokes at my ribs.

"Not much meat on this one," says the rasping voice, the words distorted as through toothless gums. "We may need to take our pleasure of it some other way."

The mad cackles redouble, their echoes a tangible pressure bearing down upon me.

I force my eyes open. It takes a few heartbeats for them to focus. When they do, it is to see a rough stone ceiling gouged from living rock. Grotesque shadows slither and dance above me.

A phlegmy sigh tickles my ear as a warm breath again bedews my cheek. Slowly, I turn my head to the side.

A witch's mask, some horrid thing carved from heartwood glares at me. Exaggerated features of hooked nose and time-creased lips, of sunken cheeks and protruding eyes make it a thing of children's nightmares. Then the mask blinks, one eye of palest blue, the other milky white. The parched lips spread into a hideous grin exposing black-stained gums devoid of teeth, save one yellowed stub in the top.

"Welcome, Hooded One," it says, then sits back to unburden my sight.

The woman—or what once was a woman—wears a gown of rarest silk, though tattered and worn so that glimpses of desiccated flesh peek through. A tarnished torc that might be silver hangs about her wattled throat. Only her hair, of purest white, shows any sign of care, neatly bound atop her skull and secured with an ivory comb.

Web of Wyrd, Urdh. The beginnings of self-doubt

"Can it not speak?" the crone asks, her mismatched eyes narrowing.

"I—" I begin to speak, but my parched throat closes on the words. I swallow what seems like dust, then manage to croak, "I thank you for your hospitality."

And like that, it is done. With the words of welcome and my acceptance, the ancient bond between host and guest forms between us. The crone smiles her horrid smile.

"Rise," she says. "Eat."

She beckons to her companions, who dutifully move to my sides. One is a comely maid, fair of complexion and with her red hair hung loose. Mischief plays in her sky-blue eyes. Were I a younger man—or simply not so rain-battered—I might ask her for a walk in the heath.

The other woman is handsome, matronly. Life has given her a certain hardiness that shows through her strong features. Silver streaks in her auburn hair tell of fires once grown hot and now turning to ash.

Five Elements, Air | Nine Worlds, Jotunheim. A hint of the innovation of Nauthiz, seen literally as fire-making

The pair help me sit up, and only then do I notice my nakedness. On reflex, I suck in my belly, gone soft of late. There's nothing I can do about the rest.

"Be at ease, son of Borr," says the eldest. "There's naught of man nor mankind we've not before witnessed."

"My daughter speaks true," says the matron, and I think either she's misspoken or I've misheard. "Would it were not so. But here. Take, drink."

She offers me a wooden bowl. My mouth floods at

the scent of venison and onions and leeks. I take the broth and sip gently at first, then in one quaff gulp down the rest.

"Now," says the youngest. She takes the bowl from my hands, her fingers warm on mine. "You have received our shelter and hospitality. What gift do you bring in exchange?"

I blink, dumbfounded. My custom is to be the host, to offer bread and meat and mead, then to receive whatever token my guest might offer in return. I cannot remember a time when I was in position to offer the thanks-gift—let alone when I had none to give.

Web of Wyrd, Odin. A call-back to the protagonist's high station

"I beg pardon of my ladies, but I have nothing to offer in return." I gesture along my naked body. "Not even the clothes off my back."

The three stare at me blankly, without rancor or pity or any emotion at all. After a couple dozen heartbeats they at last look at one another, seem to reach some unspoken accord, then turn back to me.

"If it has nothing to offer," the matron says, "it has no use. Let it join Mimir. Let it be fodder for the hogs."

No sooner has she spoken than the maiden and the crone—moving with surprising strength—pin my shoulders to the stone table. I try to resist but it feels as though lead seeps from my belly into my limbs.

The women tuck my feebly kicking feet into a coarse, black sack. They pull this over my legs, my hips, my chest.

The maiden gives me a mischievous smile. She leans toward me and kisses me, slow and deep. When she pulls away, I feel what seems to be a coin on my tongue. Before I can question her, the matron offers her lips and deposits two more coins.

Cold tendrils coil about my spine as the crone stoops toward me. I shudder as she covers my mouth with lips both parched and wet. She flicks the coins off my tongue with hers, and before I can utter my disgust, floods my mouth with more bits of metal.

The crone stands back and clamps a gnarled hand over my mouth. I can only grunt in protest as I feel my lips bind together.

"Let you not go giftless to your next host," she says.

She wipes her mouth, then with a placid smile pulls the sack over my head and cinches me into darkness.

Nine Worlds, Helheim. An inverse form of purification

Nine Worlds, Asgard. A literal callback to the Inciting Incident and the Rune of transformation

Web of Wyrd, Odin. An echo of his initial status

ROUGH HANDS GRASP my shoulders through the sackcloth and haul me across the table. Or is it a wagon bed? I hear the stamp of a hoof and the jangle of harnesses as I drop onto squelching earth. A toe nudges my ribs none too gently, and I cough a muffled protest.

"So it lives." The voice is deep and gruff.

I feel movement at the mouth of the sack and breathe a sigh of relief as light creeps in. Gentle rays become dazzling beams as the sack is upended and I sprawl into daylight. The reborn sun has yet to dry the earth, and I land elbows- and thighs-deep in rotting muck. My stomach twists, and two dozen coins pour from my mouth, brilliant gold glittering in the mud.

"Ah, my ladies have sent me coin."

A man crouches in front of me, one hand braced against a stout yew staff, the other groping in the mire. His fingers brush a coin, and he grasps it and tests the gold with his teeth.

"Fair payment," he says, and stuffs the coin in a fur pouch hanging from his belt. "Well, make yourself useful. Fetch the others for me. Mind you, I'll know if any go astray."

I'm unaccustomed to being ordered about, but nor

has this day been my usual experience. I pluck the coins from the mire. Each bears a common glyph—a spoked wheel of some sort—on one side, but a unique figure on the other.

The man snaps his fingers impatiently, and I hold my cupped and brimming hands out to him. He makes no response, so I look at him in question. My stomach twists again.

His weathered face is scored, temple to jaw, by four ragged scars, as though by the claws of some giant cat. Two of the creases pass his eyes, the now empty sockets puckered and seeping. He must sense my horrified gaze, for he raises one bisected eyebrow.

"Well?"

I shake off my bemusement, reach out, and drop the coins in his pouch. The old man listens for each clink of metal upon metal. The last coin catches on a fold of the pouch. Only when I tip it off and it gives its rattle does the man's expression relax. He gives the pouch a confirming shake, then sets his sightless gaze on me.

"Very well, then," he says. "Your ransom is paid. Now tell me, what is it you seek?"

My brow tightens at that. What I want is a warm fire and soft clothes, a pot of wine and a rasher of meat. What I want is not to be interrogated by this man.

I open my mouth to tell him as much, but he pre-empts me.

"I asked not what you want, king-made-outcast. I ask you what you seek."

His words cut through my pride, remind me of my current lot. I was a king, but now my name is Outcast. Now my brothers warm my throne, dent my bed, and—if fear be true—tup my wife.

You're meant to lead us. My memory echoes with Ve's words, my brother's cheeks red with fury as he

Nine Worlds, Jotunheim. Nauthiz (fire-starter) in the West as a sense of false comfort (air element)

Nine Worlds, Muspelheim. The awakening of the soul

Odin's Lots, Identity. The judge (agent of transformation) brought low

Five Elements, Fire. The beginning of wisdom, the first awakening of the mind

declaimed me. *Instead, you weigh down your throne, watching and judging.*

And whoring, Vili said through a mouth filled with half-chewed boar. He pointed a rib at me and grinned through flesh-strung teeth. *Don't forget the whoring. He does rest his throne to weigh down a ripe maid oft enough.*

My heart sinks at the memory, and my stomach clenches yet again. I fall back to the mud, further staining my body even as the truth stains my conscience.

I bow my face to the earth, the smells of dung and decay fit companions to my character. A sob bursts from my throat, choking off whatever words I might try to utter.

After a time, when grief and regret have loosened their strangleholds, I raise myself to my knees and sit back. The old man remains as he was—silent, expectant, demanding.

"I seek wisdom," I tell him.

A grim smile quirks the corner of his mouth.

"And what would you pay for this wisdom you seek, son of Borr?"

"All that I have," I answer without thinking.

"And what is that?" he demands. "Have you any more a kingdom? Have you lands and silver and gold?"

I bow my head, eyes fixed on my grubby hands.

"No," I say.

"No, you have not. All things require fair trade in exchange," the man says. "What you seek is perhaps the most valuable thing in all the Nine Worlds. So, what will you give in exchange for it?"

I clasp my hands and raise them toward him.

"Take my hands," I say. "Take my feet, my body, my very freedom. Take what you will, only give me wisdom."

The old man snorts a laugh at me.

"I have hands enough. And feet as well. What work

there is to be done, I am content enough to do myself. And, no, Borr's son, it is not what I would take, but what you would give."

Despair wraps its heavy cloak about me. I've offered all I have, and this impoverished pig farmer denies me? Still, he faces me expectantly, his blind eyes gazing at—

Odin's Lots, Essence. The awkening of emotion over intellect and cunning

Without a thought, I reach toward my left eye. Even as my consciousness shouts in protest, I jab a finger into my own eye socket. Pain and insanity scream from my mouth as the soft ball of jelly gives way. I pluck it from its socket and snap its tether.

The old man smiles.

"You offer a worthy gift," he says, and takes the gleaming orb from my hands.

I palm away the tears and blood that stream down my cheek. The old man taps his staff and feels his way across the cart path to a stone-walled well.

"A worthy gift indeed," he adds and, without further ceremony, drops my eye into the well.

I cry out in protest and start to rise, to scramble toward the well. But before I reach my feet a vertiginous wave crashes over me and I fall to the ground.

Countless images flood my mind, foreign and distorted and jumbled. My natural vision reports the sideways horizon, the mud-clotted earth, and a capering madman by the well. Overlying this, the mad vision of my distant left eye seems to show every other viewpoint within all the Nine Realms.

My stomach heaves, but only bile comes up. One of the visions shows a naked wretch, lying in the mire, who spits out a yellowish gob of filth. The broken man grows larger until my tormentor fills my natural sight and stoops down before me.

"What have you done?" I demand of him.

"You asked for wisdom, did you not?" he replies. "I

Five Elements, Fire. The Mind is opened. There's no going back from here.

have given you knowledge, which is the seed of wisdom."

"I can't live like this," I say.

"And how have you fared without this knowledge?" he counters. "I sense little difference in your condition now than when you first arrived. Excepting the obvious alteration." He taps beside my empty left eye.

"I'll go mad," I say, my voice scarcely above a whisper.

Nine Worlds, Vanaheim. A hint of the Boon, the reward to come

"If you like. You are, of course, free to do as you please." The old man sits back on his haunches, leaning on his staff. "If, however, you would make this a worthy sacrifice, I am willing to help you claim the rest of your boon."

"I doubt I can take much more reward," I mutter.

"And what reward do you seek, son of Borr?" he demands, his voice sharp with fury. "You, who had the world at your fingertips? You, who had the command and care of Midgard and squandered all for your ease? You make this paltry offering at my well and think you merit reward? I waste my time."

Nine Worlds, Niflheim. A call-back to Odin's status as the failed protector

The old man spits in the mud, rises, and stalks away from me.

"You turn your back on me?" I shout, some of my old, kingly fury rising to the fore. I start to stand, but the scenes before my empty eye drive me again to the ground.

Hunger. War. Misery. Injustice. Thousands upon thousands of images flood my awareness. Though fleeting, I somehow know each name, each circumstance, each hurt. I feel the dejection, the pain, the shame, as if each were my own.

Five Elements, Fire. The awkening of the mind to the shared humanity of all

"I didn't know," I say, my voice thick with sobs.

"You didn't care to know," the old man says, not unkindly, as he again stoops beside me. "But now that you do, how will you use this knowledge?"

"I would heal it," I say without thinking, and then another thought arises. "And yet..."

126

"And yet?"

"Perhaps it is not mine to heal," I say, chasing the errant notion. "Perhaps it is meet for each to experience his own journey, however torturous the path."

Nine Worlds, Vanaheim. The beginnings of true wisdom, the attaining of the Boon

"Is this the beginning of wisdom I hear?" Humor creases the corners of the old man's empty eyes.

"You said this knowledge was the beginning. Show me the rest."

Without another word, he takes me under one arm and hauls me to my feet. He is shorter than I and, though seeming frail, easily takes my weight. He guides me to the well, to the foot of a yew tree that grows beside it.

Nine Worlds, Svartalfheim. Confirmation of the Allies as those who listen to divine inspiration

"You must look up to see below," he tells me. "In abandoning that which you know shall you come to the knowing of all things."

He hands me his staff, and I then realize that one end has been sharpened and hardened in the fire. With sudden clarity I recognize what must be done.

I take the staff and awkwardly climb the yew tree. Its gnarled and twining branches form passable footholds, and I'm soon twice my height above the ground. I find a crook in the tree that will serve my purpose, secure my ankles in it, and fall back.

Nine Worlds, Ljossalfheim. First hint of the Return and the sharp directness of Tyr

From where I hang, the well looms below me. Following the old man's instructions, I bend my head back and peer into the depths. My palms begin to sweat, and I flex my fingers about the shaft of the staff-made-spear.

In dying to yourself shall you find life unending.

I grasp the shaft in both hands, draw a deep breath, and take careful aim. With a cry equal parts desperation and madness, I plunge the spear into my belly. I feel it pierce flesh and scrape bone before its tip sinks into bark and sapwood.

A wild howl fills the sky around me as all goes black.

Nothing wrong with using the physical appearance of the runes to inform the narrative

Here we meet with the accepted beginning of the myth

Nine Worlds, Svartalfheim. The return of the Allies, those who are connected to divine inspiration

True transformation—and the attainment of the boon—begins

I CANNOT TELL ALL that transpired in the time that followed my transfixion upon the great yew. In part because I am unsure of what was real and what delirium. More, because certain things may only be comprehended through the experience, and to try to understand them otherwise is as trying to catch the wind with a pitchfork.

I do know that I hung on that tree nine nights and days. Ne'er a breeze came by to cool my fevered brow or to wrest the flies from their feast on my bloodied chest and face. No food or drink came to me nor, I think, could I have tolerated them if they had. I but stared into the well, my whole eye studying the surface of the waters while my lost one surveyed all that happened in the deeps.

At some point, the three women arrived. They sat at the foot of the tree, chanting and carving strange symbols into the roots. During eight nights and days I listened to their weird, toneless song, my body wracked with pain, my soul with regret.

Only with the dawning of the ninth does my change begin to occur. From the chaos of the well order appears. A scrap of bark serves for a drinking horn. I stretch against the branches that bind my feet, against the spear that pins my body.

Eight times I reach into the well to fetch a draft of clearest water, enough for three swallows each. And each swallow cleanses my soul of rot, my mind of waste, my heart of fear. With the ninth draft, all the secrets of the well come into clarity, I fall back against the tree, screaming I draw the mysteries into my being, their fiery power coursing through my veins.

"Does it live?" the maiden asks, and the other women offer their assessments.

The old man approaches to retrieve his staff. I whimper as he twists and withdraws the shaft from my torn flesh.

"It does," the woman says, then she and her companions draw me down from the tree.

Another literal or iconic representation of the Rune within the narrative.

They set me beside the well, that deep place of all-knowing. As before, every experience within the Nine Realms floods my awareness. Now, however, their threads of cause and effect stream along with them, twisting and twining and forming clear patterns. Chaos no longer rules, but a beautiful tapestry, elegant in its balance.

Kenaz. Odin's Lots, Wound | Web of Wyrd, Skuld. The wound can now be healed with the outcome of attaining true knowledge.

"I must give this to my people," I say, and even as the words leave my mouth, I know them to be false. "I must give my experience to my people," I resolve instead, "and allow each to experience these mysteries, these Runes, for themselves."

Nine Worlds, Vanaheim. Grasping the Boon and reconizing its true value

THE SUN BURNS GENTLY in a pale blue sky. Sheep graze in the meadows alongside the road, while the farmers and their families wave to me in welcome as I pass by. A handful—the more intrepid—invite me to share a jar of ale or mead with them, to rest a while in the shade of a tree, and to offer a blessing upon hearth and steading. I oblige these and share what I can, but I daren't abide long for I have far to go.

The Ordinary World has already been righted by attaining the Boon

The sun is well toward its setting before I see the outline of my home, the spire of my keep. Half of Sunna's disk is below the horizon ere I reach the gates. My heart swells with joy for my journey's ending, yet quakes with dread at my reception.

Vili, fierce warrior and renowned hunter, guards

the path, mail and shield and spear gleaming in the waning sunlight.

"Stand aside and let me pass, little brother," I say to him.

He seems puzzled and looks dramatically about.

"Does a gnat fart?" he says. "Does a flea belch? I thought I heard something."

"Stand aside," I say again, more softly, "and let me pass."

He sticks a finger in his ear and shakes it.

"There it is again," he says. "I'd swear—"

His words end in a wheezing gurgle when I jab the tip of my staff into his throat. His spear and shield clatter to the ground as he falls to his knees, hands clasped about his neck.

I heft the mail coat over his head then slip into it myself. I leave Vili's weapons where they lie, push him onto his side with my foot, and step over him and through the gate.

Torches burn alongside the winding path to the hall. The sky shows only the memory of daylight when I reach the door and push it open.

The hall is devoid of its usual crowd, peopled only by my wife and my brother Ve, seated at the high table.

I cross the threshold, and my wolves, Gere and Freke, dart out from under the dais and rush toward me, growls deep in their throats. I do not kneel to greet them, but neither do I turn away. I simply stand as I am and look them each in the eye. Their hackles drop, ears pitch forward, then each circles about me and sits by my side.

"'Tis a foul east wind brings a stench into my hall," Ve says. "Soek, Vitr, remove this filth from these walls."

A pair of armed guards step from the shadows and move toward me. The wolves rise to stand between me and the men, ominous thunder rumbling within them.

Nine Worlds, Ljossalfheim. Tiwaz, exemplar of the Return, stands for direct action, forthrightness

The physical expression of Dagaz (the Boon) in the balancing of night and day

"You both have served me well," I tell the warriors, "and may continue to do so. Only stay in your rightful places."

The men share a glance, cast looks at the wolves, then in unspoken agreement step back into the shadows.

"You eat my bread, brother," I say as I move toward the high table. "You drink my wine. To say nothing of my..."

With strength and agility I've not felt in ages, I leap onto the waist-high dais, rest my staff, and lean upon the table.

In addition to the land, the health of our protagonist has also been restored

"Wife," I say, and nod to the lady of the hall.

"Husband," Frigg replies, then raises her wine cup to me and takes a sip.

Ve's face turns scarlet, veins standing out at neck and temple.

"You would dare—"

I slam the end of my staff between his eyes. His protest falls silent, and he slumps back in his chair. I summon servants to remove him to a comfortable seat by the hearth, then move around the table to my rightful place.

"And how was your journey?" Frigg asks, offering her hand to me.

I take it, kiss her knuckles, then claim my seat beside her and adjust my mail coat about me.

"Enlightening," I say.

She breaks off a piece of bread for me, then fills a golden cup with wine. I eat the bread and take a sip of the heady red wine.

I place my hand over hers, and she grips my fingers.

"Now," I say, "let us see to our kingdom."

The shaman arights his place and reclaims his duty to guide and heal his people

Acknowledgments

MY EXPLORATION OF THE NORSE RUNES began many years ago but took a quantum leap forward when I discovered the works of Michael William Denney, also called Mahadeva. This book and the Rune sets that accompany it are a direct outgrowth of my studies with Mike, both of the Runes themselves and of the meditation techniques through which I realized this application of them. Of course, any errors in my approach or in my interpretation of the Runes is my own.

My partners in crime at Highlands Ranch Fiction Writers were among the first to workshop the application of the Runes toward story development. Thanks to Claire L. Fishback, Nicole Greene, Michael F. Haspil, LS Hawker, and Laura Main for indulging me.

Much gratitude goes to those who supported the *Runes for Writers* IndieGoGo campaign: Claire L. Fishback, Michael F. Haspil, LS Hawker, Kristina Makansi, Peita Pateman, Simon Ponder, Wendy Terrien, and Andrew Wilson.

Hannah Robertson, Marissa DeCuir and the rest of the crew at JKS Communications were indispensable in spreading the word about this project.

Finally, the journey wouldn't mean as much or be nearly as much fun without my bride, Laura. To many more grand adventures and wondrous stories.

Recommended Resources

RUNES

Denney, Michael William. *Advanced Rune Shamanism: Harmonizing the Three Selves and Balancing the Nine Worlds*. Lexington: CreateSpace Independent Publishing Platform, 2014.
———. *Rune Divination: Language of the Gods*. Lexington: CreateSpace Independent Publishing Platform, 2013.
———. *Rune Shamanism: The Forgotten Method of Galdor*. Lexington: CreateSpace Independent Publishing Platform, 2013.

Flowers, Stephen [Edred Thorsson, pseud.]. *Futhark: A Handbook of Rune Magic*. San Francisco: Weiser Books, 1984.
———. *Runecaster's Handbook: The Well of Wyrd*. San Francisco: Weiser Books, 1999.

McCoy, Daniel. *The Viking Spirit: An Introduction to Norse Mythology and Religion*. Lexington: CreateSpace Independent Publishing Platform, 2016

Tyriel [pseud.]. *The Book of Rune Secrets*. Vancouver: Rune Secrets, 2011.

NORSE MYTHOLOGY

Crawford, Jackson, trans. *The Poetic Edda: Stories of the Norse Gods and Heroes*. Indianapolis: Hackett Publishing Company, Inc., 2015.

Sturluson, Snorri [Anthony Faulkes, trans.]. *Edda*. North Clarendon: Tuttle Publishing, 1995.

STORY CRAFT AND STRUCTURE

Brooks, Larry. *Story Engineering: Mastering the 6 Core Competencies of Successful Writing*. Cincinnati: Writer's Digest Books, 2011.

Campbell, Joseph. *The Hero with a Thousand Faces*. Novato: New World Library, 2008.

Coyne, Shawn. *The Story Grid: What Good Editors Know*. North Egremont: Black Irish Entertainment LLC, 2015.

Vogler, Christopher. *The Writer's Journey: Mythic Structure for Writers*. Studio City: Michael Wiese Productions, 2007.

RECOMMENDED WEBSITES

Jackson Crawford YouTube Channel, https://www.youtube.com/channel/UCXCxNFxw6iq-Mh4uIjYvufg

Shaman of Story YouTube Channel, https://www.youtube.com/channel/UC7fwRuf4tyCOqHlyT4oX4Cg

Michael Hauge: Story Mastery, https://www.storymastery.com/

The Thunder Wizard YouTube Channel, https://www.youtube.com/channel/UCXQ4wcKooaHflPCDNIHm8UQ

About the Author

MARC GRAHAM IS AN AUTHOR, actor, story coach, and shamanic practitioner. When not on stage, in the studio, or bound to his computer, he can be found traipsing about Colorado's Front Range with his wife and their Greater Swiss Mountain Dog.

Made in the USA
Columbia, SC
02 February 2020